The Young Artist's
Handbook

© Aladdin Books 1995

Designed and produced by
Aladdin Books Ltd
28 Percy Street
London W1P 0LD

First published in The United States by
Shooting Star Press Inc
230 Fifth Avenue
Suite 1212
New York, New York 10001

The CIP data for this
book is available in
The Library of Congress

Printed in Czech Republic

ISBN 1-57335-144-X

Contents

The Young Artist's
Handbook

Written by Anthony Hodge
Illustrations by Ron Hayward Associates

CHAPTER ONE: DRAWING

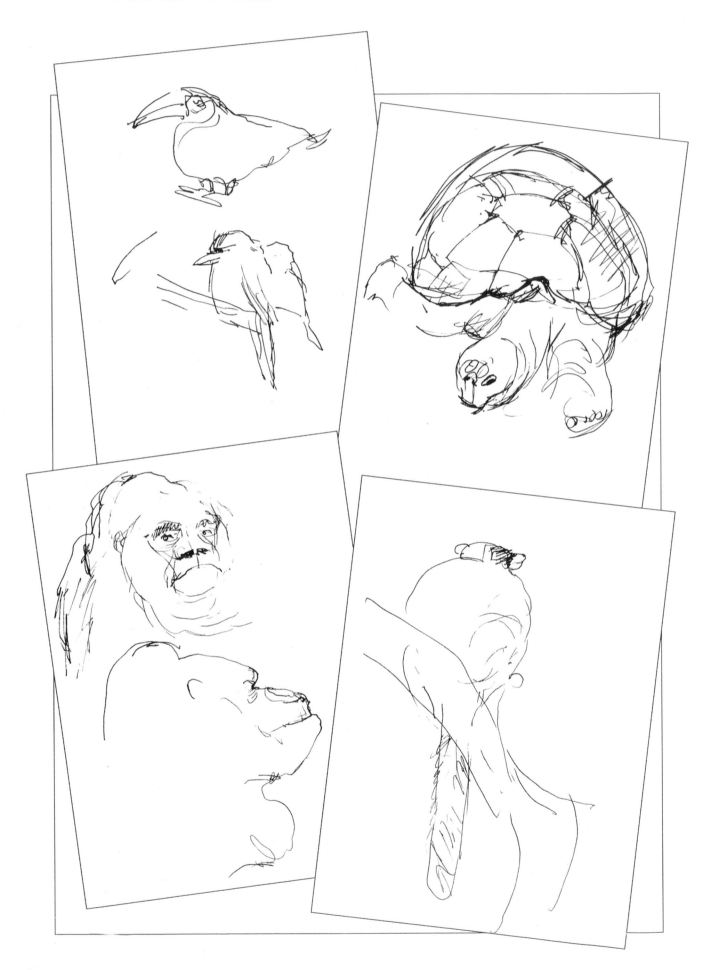

Drawing has a wonderful quality of immediacy, of something that is happening *now*. Its great advantage is that it can be done almost anywhere. With a sketch pad and pencil you need never be bored.

Starting with basics

This book aims to develop in you the natural talents and ideas that make every artist unique. We begin by examining the range of materials available. We look at some of the basic skills of drawing. Then these skills are used in a series of projects. We will explore sketching techniques and work up to more finished drawings. We will examine how simple forms can be developed into more complex ones such as the human figure. The main emphasis is on drawing what you see, but there are also projects that involve working from photographs and from your imagination.

Making connections

There are no hard and fast rules about how to draw, so try not to be too critical of your work. Drawing is about looking carefully and developing an understanding of what you see. It is an exhilarating way of feeling connected to the world.

▷ *"On the opposite page you can see some sketches I made at the zoo, using a black felt-tip pen. Whatever you feel about animals being kept in captivity, zoos are a wonderful place to draw."*

PENCIL, PEN AND WASH

Drawing involves making marks and there are plenty of different drawing tools you can use to do this. All drawing materials are made of particles of color, or *pigment*, bound together with a different kind of gum, or *medium*, to perform different jobs. These first pages are about getting to know the tools and experimenting with as many as possible.

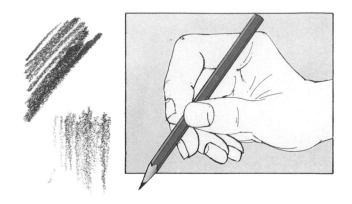

What feels most comfortable?

You will find some tools suit you more than others. Many people feel safer with a pencil than with a brush full of ink, as they feel they have less control with ink. Later on you may come to enjoy the hit and miss element of drawing with a brush, too.

Getting equipped

Gather together as many different kinds of mark-making tools as you can. It is not always necessary to buy expensive, new equipment. Keep a lookout for any unwanted bits and pieces that friends or relatives may have. The projects that appear later in this book are made in materials that are appropriate to the subject or style of the work. But there is no reason why you shouldn't use a different tool if you prefer, when you come to try them.

Pencils

Pencils are the basic drawing implement and you can produce all sorts of marks with a few pencils. Within the wooden tube of a pencil is the pigment, graphite, mixed with the medium, clay. Pencils are graded and numbered according to the hardness of the graphite. A graphite pencil marked HB is a good all-purpose tool. For a thicker, softer line, you can use anything from a 2B to a 6B.

4B

2B

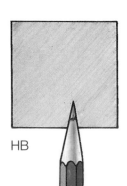
HB

2H

4H

Pen and ink

India ink is a good, strong, black medium and can be used with a drawing pen, or fountain pen, or with a brush. Drawing pens can use many different nibs. A wide range of **felt-tip pens** is also on the market. Their range of expression is limited because the mark that they make is unvarying. Modern alternatives to the ink pen include the **Rotring pen**, used for technical drawing.

Pen and wash

To make a wash you need a brush that will hold plenty of ink and water. First make a drawing with pen and ink, and let it dry. There are two kinds of ink, permanent or waterproof ink, and nonwaterproof ink. If your drawing is in nonwaterproof ink, when you wet it again the lines will run. If your drawing is in permanent ink, the hard pen lines will contrast with the soft shadows of the wash.

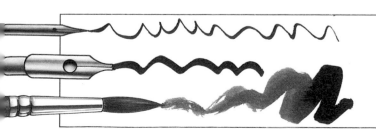

Nibs

Nibs for ink pens vary in size and thickness and, of course, the lines they make vary accordingly. Marks can also be made in ink with a paint brush.

CHARCOAL, CONTÉ AND CRAYON

Getting a grip

How you hold your drawing implement makes a big difference to the kind of line you produce. In general, if you hold your implement in the middle in a relaxed way, your arm muscles will relax, and the line you produce will be relaxed, too. If you hold your implement near the point, you can get harder, more intense marks. Try holding it at the end, to produce freer, looser marks.

Sharpening your pencils

Pencils and crayons can be sharpened with a pencil sharpener or with a sharp knife, preferably one with a safe, retractable blade. You can also use sandpaper to vary the point you get: a sharp point for thin, fine lines, and a flat edge for broad, thick lines.

Getting some support

Even if you buy your drawing paper in a pad, it may not be stiff enough to give you proper support by itself. You will need to rest your paper on a board of some kind. You can get one from an art store, or simply buy a piece of plywood or fiberboard from a hardware store.

Charcoal

Charcoal is made from burnt wood, usually willow, and is always black. It is available in sticks of various thicknesses, which are brittle and can tend to break. Charcoal is also available in *compressed* form, in a straight, hard stick, or in pencil form, encased in a paper cylinder that you can gradually tear away.

Fixative

Finished drawings, especially charcoal and pastel ones, need to be protected from smudging. This can be done by spraying them lightly with fixative.

Erasers

There are many different kinds of erasers. For chalk or charcoal drawing, it is best to use a kneaded eraser, a soft gray eraser that you can squeeze like clay into any shape you want.

Conté

Conté is a hard form of pastel compressed into a thin stick. It comes traditionally in black, white, and shades of brown, although other colors are now available. Drawing with brown rather than black conté can produce a softer, warmer drawing. Conté can be blended by rubbing it with your finger.

Wax crayon

Crayons are bold, simple sticks of color that come in many forms and prices. They can sometimes be dissolved with turpentine or mineral spirits, and applied with a brush or even with cotton. Used on a textured surface, crayons produce a grainy effect that can add considerable interest to your drawings.

What kind of paper?

Cartridge paper is fine for most pencil or ink drawings. Try out other kinds too, including colored paper. Textured paper is good for use with pastel, crayon and charcoal.

COLORED PENCIL AND PASTEL

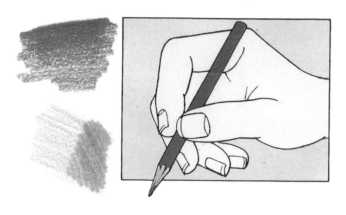
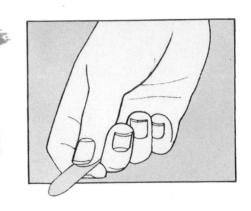

Colored pencils

Colored pencils are one of the most basic coloring tools. Many bright and wonderful colors are available. Artists like David Hockney frequently choose to use them. Although they are often used as colors in their own right, they mix and can be laid down on top of one another to achieve different effects.

Chalk pastels

Chalk pastels are pure pigment bound together with gum. They blend well if you rub them with your finger – this is messy, but effective. Pastel can be put on smoothly with the side of the chalk, or quite thickly if you press firmly with the end. As with most drawing materials, price and quality vary.

Colored pencil and wash

Water-soluble pencils are fun to experiment with. Lines drawn with them will blur to make an area of flat color if you lay a wash of clean water over them with a paint brush.

COLOR THEORY

The six colors you can see in the color wheel on the left are divided into two groups. Red, yellow and blue are called the *primary* colors. Orange, green and purple are the *secondary* colors, and are a mix of the two primaries on either side. In fact nearly all colors can be mixed from the primaries; some ways of mixing colors are shown below. The more colors are mixed together, the duller they become. The colors that are opposite each other on the color wheel are known as *complementaries*. When placed side by side, they bring out the best in each other. For example, red looks redder next to green, and vice versa.

△ **"Make a color wheel for yourself with the primary and secondary colors. Then try again, blending the secondaries from your primary colors."**

Colors can be mixed in various ways. In *cross-hatching*, shades of colored pencil are laid on top of each other.

Colors appear darker or lighter, depending on how hard you press down with your pencil or crayon.

Strokes of yellow wax crayon laid over blue produce a light green. Blue laid over yellow makes a darker green.

Wax crayons can be blended with a finger. If colors are rubbed too much, they will get dirty.

Felt-tip colors can be blended by overlapping groups of tiny dots. This technique is used in color printing.

13

BASICS: LINE, TONE AND TEXTURE

"The artist," declared Picasso, "must find a way to convince people of the complete truth of his lies." Like a conjuror, the artist uses tricks to convince us of the reality of what he shows us. The next pages cover some of these basic tricks. Line, tone and texture are three of the most important.

Starting off
The project here is to try out line, tone and texture separately. Then you can combine them in a single drawing. Find a subject you want to explore using these three techniques. You may wish to work from a photograph of your pet or your favorite animal, perhaps.

Taking a line for a walk
Lines are used to describe the shape of objects. By varying the thickness of your lines you can show all that is necessary to capture your subject.

White paper is part of your picture
Notice how the different approaches affect the white paper that you are working on. In the line drawing, the lines enclose areas of white paper, which become shapes in their own right. In the tone drawing, much of the paper is covered with a tone of some kind. The areas of white represent the lightest tone. In the texture drawing, the white areas form an important contrast with the marks that cover the rest of the paper.

A lot can be left to the imagination, which can fill in what is missing.

Showing light and dark
The tone of an object is its darkness or lightness relative to other things. The cat in the middle picture below is darker than the rug, which is a lighter tone. But the tone of an object also changes depending on how light falls on it. Selective shading of parts of your drawing can be used to indicate these variations in tone, as shown in the picture top right.

Line

What is it made of?

If your drawings have texture, they will be rich, varied, and exciting to look at. The texture of your pencils or crayons on rough paper also helps to convey the actual texture of your subject, like the hairiness of the cat or the coarseness of the rug in the picture bottom right.

"As you can see from my examples, the drawings for this project can be kept simple. It is not necessary to make your drawings complex, until you try in your final one (mine is top right) to combine all three techniques in a single image."

Tone

Texture

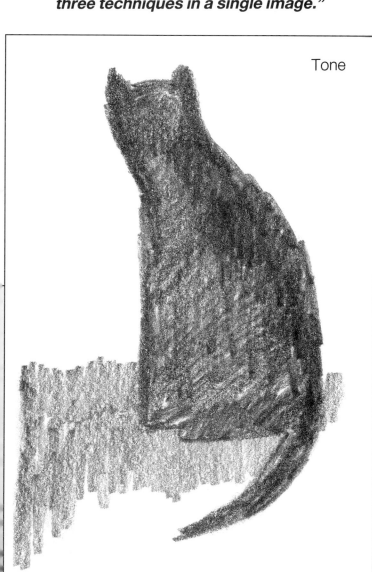

BASICS: FINDING THE FORM

An artist sometimes stalks his or her subject, moving in on it as gradually as a hunter moves in on his prey. It is not always possible to get things right the first time. Sometimes it is necessary to work in a very general way at first and only gradually approach the finished result.

Feeling your way

For this project, choose a simple object, such as a tin can or a box. Put it on the table in front of you and look at it carefully. Take a pencil and

begin by sketching it loosely. Go over and over your drawing with very soft lines until the shape you want begins to appear. Be very free at this stage as all mistakes can be erased later. Gradually feel your way toward the finished drawing.

Drawing with X ray eyes

Try to think of your subject as transparent, so that you draw what you know to be there as well as what you can see. In the first drawing below, all of the bottom of the tin can is drawn in, although only part can be seen. At the second stage the form of the tin can becomes clearer. Tones begin to be indicated.

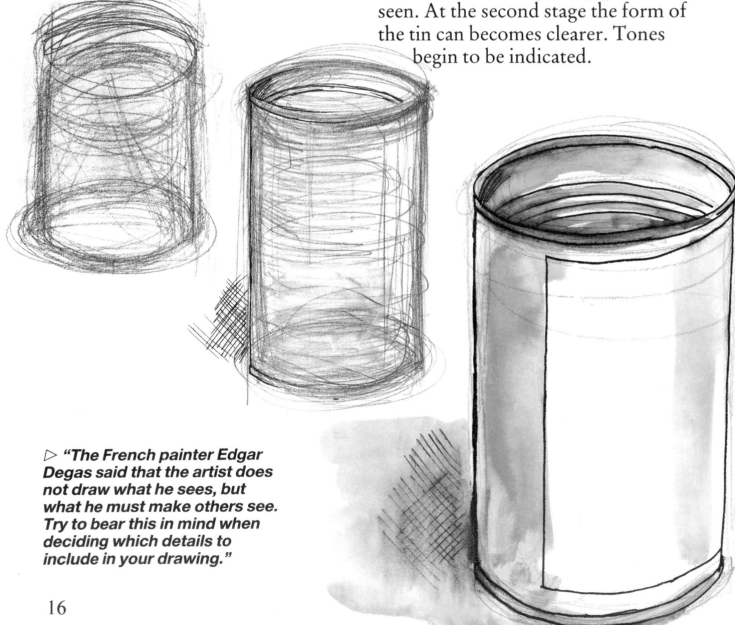

▷ *"The French painter Edgar Degas said that the artist does not draw what he sees, but what he must make others see. Try to bear this in mind when deciding which details to include in your drawing."*

Drawing to a conclusion

Once you have got the basic form more or less right, start to notice how the light falls on it and where shadows appear. The last stage can be done with a soft pencil which produces a dark line, with dark crayon, conté, or pastel, or with pen and ink. If you use pen and ink for the final drawing, you can rub out the pencil lines once the ink has dried.

Try different kinds of shading techniques to convey the texture and tone of your subject. Cross-hatching, dots, and lines running around the form can all help to convey the shape and character of your subject, as shown in the final drawing.

Practicing forms

Drawing can become second nature. The more you practice, the easier it becomes. Once you are familiar with this way of drawing, you can go on to do anything you like in the same way. Practice this method on other simple forms, like the ones that appear below. You can decide for yourself how much detail to put in.

Don't forget that sometimes you can overdraw. You will probably have to overwork a few drawings to find the right moment to stop. Remember that a fresh and lively drawing is often more interesting to look at than one that is overworked and labored.

The basic three-dimensional forms

From the pyramid, sphere, cylinder, cube and cone pictured here, more complex shapes can be built. Most of what we see around us can be drawn from these simple beginnings. Make a collection of objects from around your home that are similar to, or based on, these forms. Practice drawing these shapes, which form the basis for many of the other projects in this book.

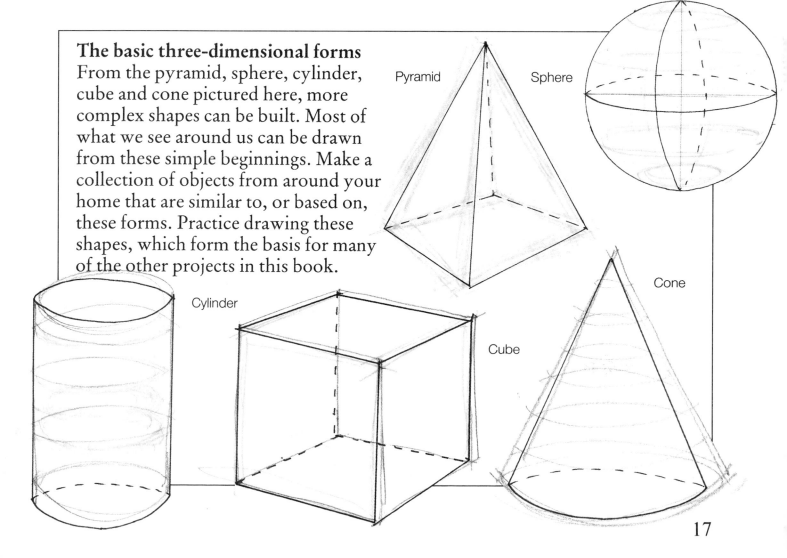

Pyramid

Sphere

Cylinder

Cube

Cone

BASICS: LIGHT AND SHADE

Imagine drawing a bowl of fruit and making it so lifelike that people feel hungry just looking at it! This may seem a tall order, but it is possible with a bit of practice to give your drawings a real depth and solidity. One of the keys to this is the use of light and shade.

When you were drawing the form on the previous page, you began to notice the play of light and shadow on it. Everything has a light and a dark side, and usually a part which is in between the two.

Throwing light on the subject

Take the subject of your previous project and a flashlight, or a lamp whose beam of light you can direct. Light up your object and study the shadows. You'll notice one shadow on the side of the object itself, making it look solid, and one that is the shadow cast by the object onto the surface on which it is standing.

Be a town planner

Most of what we see around us in the world is made up of simple shapes.

There is no light without shadow
Make a collection of objects based on the forms on the previous page. You might include a ball, a tin can and a box. Shine a light on them and practice seeing and drawing the forms with their shadows. Move your source of light around and watch the shadows change. The effects are demonstrated below in black and gray felt-tip pen. The gray areas show the middle or *half-tone*.

Although an object generally gets darker as less light falls on it, there is often a lighter part just before the outer edge. This is because light has bounced back from another surface (the table on which the objects have been placed, for example). It lights the object from behind. This is reflected light. With shiny objects, like glass or tin, light is reflected from many angles.

These may be built into complicated forms. Use your imagination and invent a picture in which the shapes come together. Imagine you have been asked to design a new town. Think of all the shapes of buildings you could design using the basic forms. What kind of vehicles can you picture driving through the streets?

Where is your sun?
Draw in the outlines of your forms first. Then decide where the sun is (it may not actually appear in your drawing, but the effects of it will). The position of the sun determines where the shadows fall and how long they are. As the sun goes down, shadows get longer. When you have finished, look and see how real buildings in sunlight compare with the ones you have drawn. Yours may be better designed!

▽ *"In my felt-tip drawing the sun appears quite low in the sky, and casts long shadows. Windows and other details can make your sketch more interesting."*

BASICS: PERSPECTIVE

Perspective is a means of creating a feeling of space in your drawings. It is a way of trying to represent the three-dimensional world on a flat piece of paper. To achieve this sense of space, you must establish the proper place on paper for things that are close to you and those that are far away. Things that are near must appear to advance toward you on paper, and things that are further away should be seen to go back, or *recede*, in your drawing, too.

Do we need rules?

Sevderal hundred years ago in Renaissance Italy, artists laid down a set of rules which helped to show perspective. Some artists understand these rules and make use of them. Some understand the rules and choose to ignore them; like the late Henri Matisse, a famous Fauve artist. The rules are given here so you can understand them and decide if you wish to use them.

A great deal has been written about the theory of perspective. But the best way of practicing it is to observe your surroundings carefully and put down on paper the things you notice.

Three techniques

In drawing there are three main techniques for showing perspective. They appear in the main picture and are described on the opposite page. Get to know and practice each of them separately before trying the project, which is to put them together in a more complex picture. Some subjects are more suited to one technique than another.

▷ *"My main drawing shows the three techniques in combination. The figures show the technique of overlapping. The street is shown to recede into the background through the use of linear perspective. Tones and textures are more pronounced in the foreground, so this area looks closest to us."*

Linear

Overlapping

Tonal

The secrets of perspective

The examples on the left show the three main ways of showing perspective. The first is linear perspective. In this technique, lines that in fact run parallel to one another appear to meet on a point on the horizon known as vanishing point.

The second detail demonstrates the technique of overlapping. When one object is in front of another, the object in front hides part of the one behind. Test out this theory by looking around you and making drawings of your own.

The third technique is tonal perspective. Strong, dark marks will separate the front or foreground of a drawing from the softer lines of the background. So differences in tone can make parts of a drawing seem closer or further away.

BASICS: COMPOSITION

There is something to be said for the idea of making drawings of things as you find them. Composition, however, is about rearranging things and ordering them in a new way that seems more balanced and harmonious. In this project you can test this out for yourself.

The artist Paul Cézanne used to spend hours setting up his still-life subjects, even using coins to tip up bowls and jars so he could see inside more easily. By the time he had started work on a picture, he had practically finished! His subject already looked exactly as he wanted it to in the final work. How did he know what he wanted?

What feels right for you?
A good feel for composition can be developed by creating your own picture by trial and error. Make a collection of household objects.

A composition is a group of colored shapes in certain positions. Try some unlikely ones, even those that you know will look peculiar. Experiment with a series of arrangements on a tabletop or even on the floor. Try out compositions that you think will look unbalanced in some way: top-heavy, cramped, or too spaced out, as well as ones that look balanced. Unorthodox compositions sometimes produce good results.

Which way up?
Your drawing paper has a particular shape. You can, of course, decide which way up to hold it, making a picture that is wide or tall. Before you begin, spend some time imagining how each arrangement will look on paper.

Choose ones you feel might go well together in a picture. In the examples below there are five, but you might like to start with more. You could then discard some as you go along, if you find they don't fit in.

Trying out composition
Rearrange your objects and make a series of drawings based on them. Test out the idea that a harmonious or pleasing composition is a balanced one. In a balanced composition, a single large object can appear to equal two smaller ones. Perhaps you could have one or more of the objects only partially in your picture. Many artists have used this technique deliberately, to make unexpected compositions.

▽ *"Compositions can look orderly, comfortable, or plain crazy! My three examples here are quite sensible, but you don't have to be!"*

DRAWING THE HEAD

Our faces tell a lot about who we are and how we are feeling, whether we like it or not. Over the next pages we will examine how to draw them step by step, looking at the proportions of the head, the features, and finally, how to achieve a likeness.

The shape of the head
Viewed from the front, the head is an egg-shaped form sitting on the cylinder of the neck. From the side, it is helpful to see the head as two overlapping eggs, and the three-quarter view is the same, only with the second egg more hidden. These views are illustrated below. Practice drawing the shape of the head and positioning the features within it as described in the box below. Use the method described on pages 16-17 to feel your way toward the form and proportions of the head.

A study from life
When you are confident that you can manage these proportions, ask a friend to sit for you. Perhaps you can draw each other at the same time; or you may prefer to try a self-portrait. Make drawings of your subject's head from side, front and three-quarter views. Don't worry about getting a perfect likeness at this stage.

▷ *"My simple line drawing could be taken further by adding shading, but I felt it might become confused. Sometimes it's best to quit while you are ahead, rather than risk going on for too long."*

Making the headlines
The proportions of the head are shown here. The first thing to notice is that the eyes come halfway down the head, and not higher up. The end of the nose lies midway between eyes and chin; the mouth comes halfway between nose and chin. There is the width of an eye between the eyes, and also across the bottom of the nose. On the sides of the head, the ears should be placed midway between the eyes and the nose.

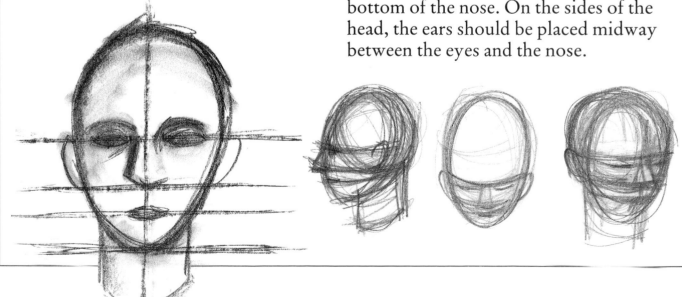

FEATURES AND EXPRESSIONS

We all have in common two eyes and ears, a nose, and a mouth. These features may conform to certain shapes: the nose is a triangular form, eyes are oval in shape. But no two people's features are ever exactly the same, even if they are related.

On the opposite page, the different features are drawn step by step. The first drawing in each sequence shows the basic form. The second shows the individual character developing, and in the third, shadow has been added to emphasize the form.

A subject for your portrait

When you are familiar with drawing features and expressions, it's time to try to achieve a likeness. This is fun as long as no one minds whether you succeed or not. When Oliver Cromwell had his portrait painted, he insisted that he was shown "warts and all." The artist was lucky on this occasion, as people can be sensitive about how they look! If you find it difficult to get someone to pose, try drawing from a photograph of someone you know or admire.

Getting a likeness

A likeness depends on drawing the features and capturing how they combine together. The rest of the face is almost as important as the features. The distance between the eyes, or the gap between nose and mouth, vary as much as the shape of the nose. In a portrait it's important to get these details right.

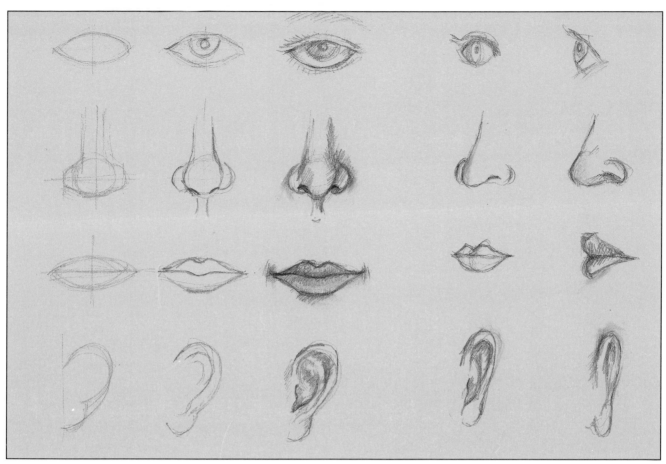

△ *"Above I have sketched front, side and three-quarter views of the same features. Cross-hatching has added solidity."*

Putting on expressions

The drawings on the left show the subject of the previous page in different moods: first sad, then happy, and finally just puzzled. The features and even the hair droop downward in the sad face, as if there is no energy to keep them up. Enthusiasm lifts the lines upward in the happy face. In a puzzled face, the lines are undecided and waver in different directions. Try out these expressions yourself in a mirror and feel how the muscles in your face move. See how your face changes as you practice looking delighted, annoyed or tired.

THE HUMAN FIGURE

When the American space program launched the rocket, *Pioneer 10,* into outer space, in June of 1983, they attached a plaque to inform extra-terrestrials about the planet Earth. The plaque featured a drawing of two figures – a man and a woman. It's strange to think that other beings might look very different to us. Imagine that you've been given the task of showing aliens what humans are like. You will need to show the body in proportion.

Getting things in proportion

Proportion is about comparing the size of one thing to another. For the artist, it is about showing different sizes correctly on paper. The drawings on the right show the proportions of the human figure. The length of the body is often measured in relation to the head. The average adult, whether male or female, is seven heads tall. The torso is three heads long from the chin to the top of the legs, and divides into thirds at the nipple line and navel. The distance from the top of the legs to the soles of the feet also measures three heads. Children's heads are larger in proportion to the rest of their bodies. Adult or child, with your arms stretched out sideways, the distance between your fingertips measures the same as your height – try it!

Foreshortening

Here the story gets more complicated; these proportions appear to change as we move about. Parts of the body appear larger or smaller, depending on whether they are near or far from the person looking at them. We found out about this in the project on perspective.

If someone's leg or arm is pointing directly at you, part of its length will be hidden. This is known as *foreshortening.* You can see it on the right in the drawings of the figures sitting and crouching, and also in the sketches at the bottom of the opposite page.

Practicing foreshortening

Foreshortening takes a more dramatic turn when you look at the figure from an unusual angle. As shown in the drawings left and middle opposite, a person with his arm outstretched toward you, or lying down, will seem to have an enormous hand or enormous feet. Have a go at drawing someone in these positions. It takes a lot of practice to get these things to look right, but you can have fun on the way as long as you don't mind making mistakes. The third picture is a sketch of the artist looking down at his own body and drawing himself at work. Try it. If you shut one eye, you can even see your nose, and include it in the picture, as he did.

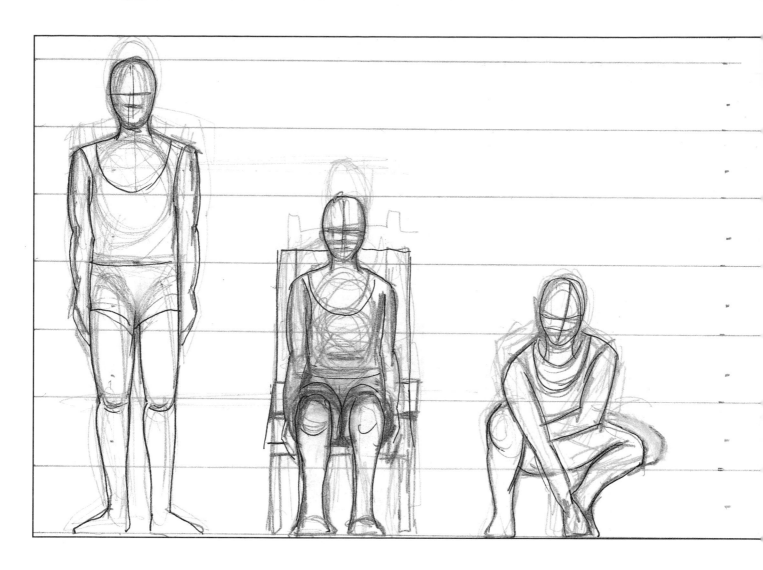

△ "Above I have drawn the proportions of the standing figure. You might want to copy this first. Try it again from memory, and then check the measurements against a real person."

△ "The seated figure shows how two heads have been 'lost' from the height; the space from hips to knees has become foreshortened. Again, check this against the real thing."

△ "The crouching figure is more complicated, as the top half is also foreshortened as it leans toward you. The legs are foreshortened differently. Can you see how?"

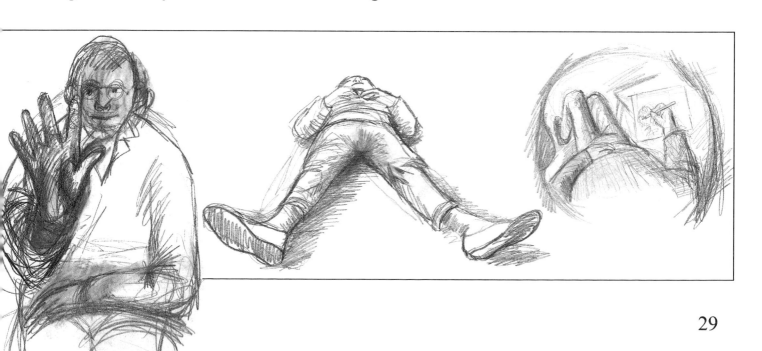

PEOPLE ON THE MOVE

"Don't try to run before you can walk," the saying goes, and it's true that if you overreach yourself in the real world, you fall and hurt yourself. However, in a world of flat paper, if we take a risk that doesn't come off, we are none the worse for it.

A sense of balance

You can learn a lot about how the figure moves by trying it yourself! As you walk or run, practice being aware of what happens to your body. Feel how the weight shifts from one leg to the other, so that each leg in turn holds the body up as the other swings forward to take the next step. Try squatting down and feel how your weight is distributed.

Let's get moving

We take walking and running for granted, but we all had to learn how to balance. The illustrations below show a figure running. Each part of the sequence flows into the next.

Notice how at each stage, the running figure is balanced by the different positions of the limbs.

The project takes this idea further. Find a photograph of someone running, an athlete perhaps, in a newspaper or magazine. Photographs can be confusing, so choose one where you can really see what's happening. Make a drawing based on the photograph you have chosen.

Before and after

Before photographs were invented, artists had to rely on their eyes and their imagination. The next step is to try to imagine the positions the runner would be in before and after the photograph was taken. Make sketches of these positions on either side of your first drawing.

Having finished the project, try drawing people on the move around you. Get used to working quickly and you will be surprised how your drawing can improve.

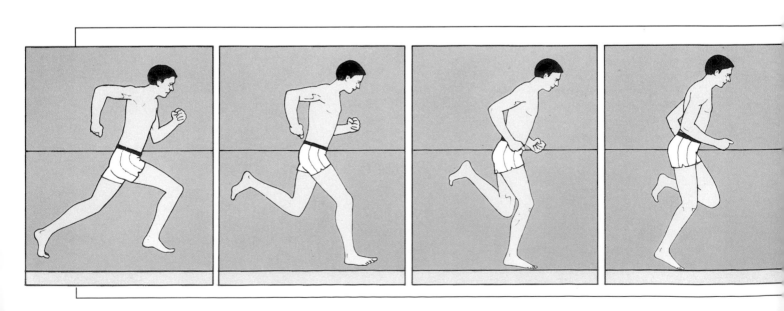

△ *"Here is an example of this project with my attempts at guessing 'before and after' positions for my runner. I've tried to get a feeling of energy and movement into the drawings so that, unlike the photograph I drew from, my sketches aren't frozen and still. Try it yourself and see how well you can do!"*

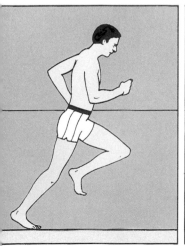
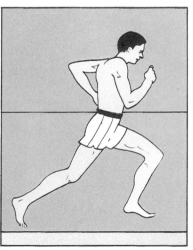

A man on the run
The illustrations of the running man are included for information, rather than as examples of how you should draw. They give a clear explanation of what happens when we run. However, your drawings should try to convey not only information, but a sense of movement too. Try making your pencil move across the paper enthusiastically, to show the runner's energy.

ANIMAL STUDIES

The variety in the world of nature provides a constant source of wonder and excitement to the artist. From camels to crocodiles, from bats to bulls, animals provide a wonderful opportunity to experiment with lines and mark-making.

The texture of an animal's coat is particularly important. Let your eyes enjoy the softness of cats, the roughness of dogs, the sleekness of horses, and the prickliness of porcupines.

Back to basics
"Treat nature by means of the cylinder, sphere and cone," said the artist Paul Cézanne.

◁ *"In this example you can see how a drawing can 'evolve,' or be built up gradually. The basic shapes develop step by step into a particular horse. At each stage, more detail is added until, finally, the animal has its own special presence. Make your own version of this sequence of drawings all in one go. You might want to put the figure of a rider on the horse's back to make your drawing more interesting."*

▽ *"In the final stages, I added tone to make my horse look more solid and to complete my picture."*

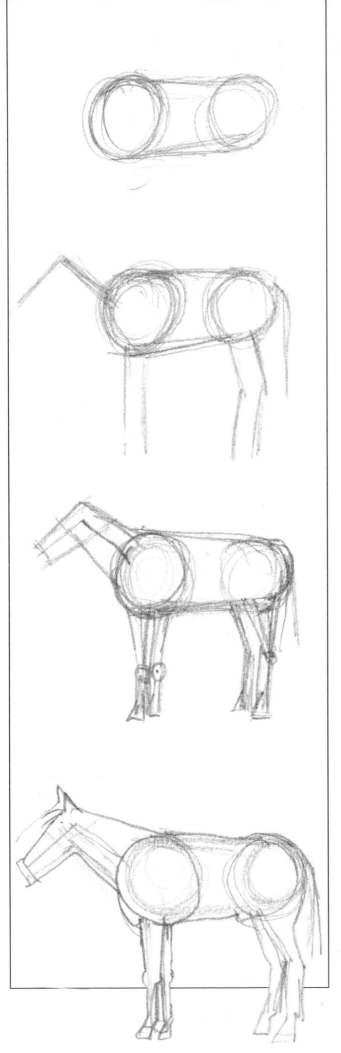

The simple shapes we studied earlier are the basis for animal forms, and can be used to make your drawings look convincing. The drawings on the left show how the figure of a horse evolves from a few basic shapes. Try this out with your own drawing and then try a similar method with other animals. What basic shapes might develop into a cow, a dog or a cat?

Animals don't stay still
What all living creatures have in common is that they move and won't pose for you. As with a moving human figure, however, the combination of photographs, your imagination and, most important, your eyes, can work very well.

Field studies
Don't be afraid to draw from real life whenever possible. Even if your drawing doesn't have a textbook likeness, it may well have a special quality about it. There is nothing so exciting for the artist as confronting the real thing armed only with a pencil and pad. Use a rough sketch book; the less expensive the better, so you will not feel that what you do has to be perfect. Learn to draw quickly and directly, and your pictures will take on a life of their own.

Caught on the hop
Below you can see an example of how an animal moves. When drawing animals in motion, it is important to let your subject draw itself for you. Look at the animal and allow your pencil to follow the forms in front of you without looking at the paper.

Make a sequence of drawings as the animal moves. When it changes position, don't be frustrated. Keep the same drawing going if it is only a slight change. If your subject changes into a different pose entirely, begin another drawing. Return to the previous one when the original pose is taken up again.

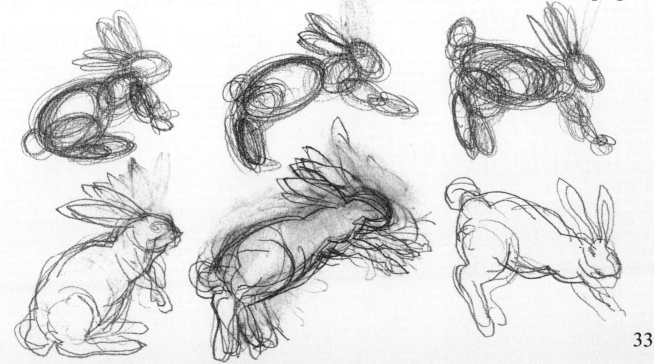

PRESENTATION

Finished drawings, particularly ones in charcoal, conté or pastel, should be sprayed with fixative to protect them and prevent them from smudging. Use fixative in a well ventilated room and be careful not to get any in your eyes. Try to spray your drawing as evenly as possible.

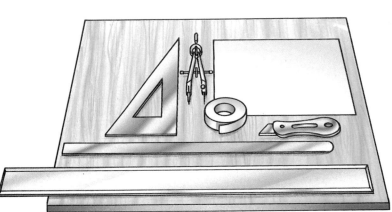

For the record
Keep a record of when your drawings were made by putting the date on them, and possibly also the place where they were made. One day you will look back with interest and notice how your work has changed over the years.

Mounting your work
Mats play an important part in the presentation process. Mounting your drawings can make them look better than you ever thought possible. In general, steer away from brightly colored mats; white and cream mats are usually effective. Measure the area for your mat accurately with a ruler, and cut it out carefully with a knife.

Drawing with a mat
Mats can also be used in the drawing process itself if you are using brush and ink, or if you are working very freely with any material. Before you begin, place a mat on your paper, framing the area in which you intend to draw. Allow your drawing to go over the edges of the mat. When you have finished, remove the mat. You will find a clean edge framing your work which will make it look smart.

PRACTICAL TIPS ON DRAWING

Keeping equipment safe

Protecting your drawing equipment is important. Keep your paper, pencils and drawing pads together in one place. This will help from a practical point of view, and give you a feeling of continuity in your work. Keep your paper in a drawer where it can lie flat and will not get creased or soiled.

Drawing large and free

Try drawing on a large scale. Don't feel that your work has to be small and detailed. You may find that you are able to express yourself more completely if you can move your arm freely. If you are the sort of person who likes working on large drawings, you may find it easier to draw standing up at an easel. Art stores stock these in various shapes and sizes. There is also a piece of equipment called a horse, which enables you to sit and work at a drawing board at the same time.

More about paper

There are many different kinds of paper, from newsprint to handmade paper. Experiment with as many sorts as possible, but don't feel you have to rely on expensive equipment all the time. The French artist Pierre Bonnard used to do most of his drawings on the backs of old envelopes! Expensive equipment can sometimes inhibit you from working freely.

Watercolor paper has a texture which is fun to work on, particularly in pastel, conté, crayon or charcoal. Its rough surface will make your strokes look broken and bold. Charcoal paper has a delicate ribbed surface.

It allows you to blend your strokes and create velvety tones.

Drawing with an eraser

An eraser can also be used as a drawing tool in its own right. It is used to introduce highlights into areas of dark tone. Try this for yourself: shade in an area of your paper with pencil or charcoal. Then draw with your eraser and reveal the white paper again. You have effectively drawn in the areas you would usually leave out. If your eraser gets dirty, rub it clean on a spare scrap of paper.

Drawing outside

Drawing outdoors can be very rewarding, but presents its own set of problems. You need to find a comfortable spot to sit, from where your subject is clearly visible. If your position becomes too cramped, your drawing is likely to suffer. If it is windy you will need to tape your paper down, or restrain it with clips. If your paper is in direct sunlight, its brightness may dazzle you. Hold your sketch pad so that your page is in the shade.

Getting ideas

Keep a scrapbook of images cut from newspapers and magazines as possible subject matter for future work.

Visit art galleries whenever you can, and learn from the work displayed there. A great deal about cross-hatching and other techniques can be learned from etchings in museums. Carry a pocket-size sketch book around with you for noting down ideas, and making quick sketches for later use.

CHAPTER TWO: PAINTING

△ "Here is a detail from a seascape I painted at Newlyn Harbor in Cornwall, England. Even when you paint from life, it's important to feel free to experiment and bring in ideas from your imagination. If an impulse comes to you, go along with it and see where it leads you. Some of the best ideas arrive from nowhere, so keep an open mind, relax and above all, be sure to enjoy yourself."

"An artist is not a special kind of person, but every person is a special kind of artist." A. Coomaraswamy, writer and artist.

This chapter provides an introduction to a series of ideas and techniques that will help you express yourself in paint. Painting is an area in which everyone can be of equal value, because each person's work is unique. Some of you have an eye for detail; others form a general impression of the world. These differences will be reflected in how you paint.

Freedom to experiment

The projects in this book cover a wide range of different kinds of painting. One project leads on to the next. We will start with tools and materials, color-mixing and other practical skills. Later a series of projects will introduce ways of using these techniques, bringing in your own ideas.

What you need

Before you begin, you will need to be wearing old clothes which may get splashed with paint. You will also need newspaper or an old sheet to cover the surface on which you work, and somewhere to put your work while it dries. Clean your brushes thoroughly with water when you finish using them. If you use oil paint, you will need turpentine and rags, followed by soap and water, to clean your brushes when you finish.

TOOLS AND MATERIALS

Most paintings are done with brushes, but there are many other ways paint can be applied. In the picture you can see a few examples and you may be able to think of more. Make a collection of brushes and other mark-making implements and get ready for an experimental session with them.

A good palette is an especially important tool, to mix your colors on. It must be large enough to carry plenty of paint, and have room left over for unexpected extra color-mixing. A wooden palette from the art supply store is a good investment, as it is seasoned wood and can be cleaned easily. Otherwise plastic or another nonabsorbent surface will do.

Poster paint is a cheap form of gouache. It comes in pots or paint boxes. Make sure you get plenty of color on your brushes.

Which paint suits you best?
Colors are made of *pigments* (colored powders), most of which are mined from the ground and mixed with various binding materials to perform different jobs. You may find one kind of paint or *medium* suits you so well that you use it all the time, or you may like to keep changing from one to another. Other kinds of paints not featured here are emulsion, tempera and gloss.

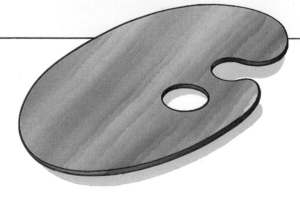

Acrylic is a paint made of plastic. It can be used thin like watercolor or thick like oil. It dries quickly, so don't squeeze out too much.

Surfaces to paint on

The paintings in this book are mostly in acrylic on white paper or cardboard. Acrylic can be used on most things. Oil paint will sink into most surfaces if they haven't been prepared with a *primer* like gesso or size. Try using oil on hardboard, canvas, cardboard and plywood; get off-cuts from local stores. Don't spend all your money in the art supply store – expensive equipment can stop you working in a relaxed way.

Watercolor is transparent, and should be used on white paper. The paper needs to be taped down or it will wrinkle up.

Gouache is mixed with water but is not transparent. It is finely ground which means it is good for detailed work and illustration.

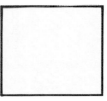

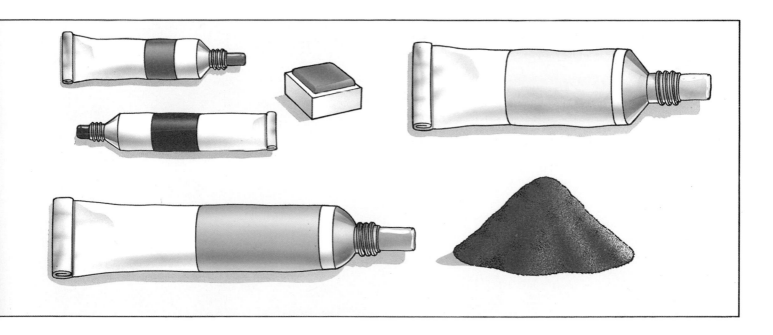

Oil paint can be used thick or thin and can be diluted or *thinned* with turpentine. It usually takes a long time to dry.

Powder paint is sometimes used in schools. It's good for large pictures as it's not too expensive to buy.

FEELING YOUR WAY

An important part of painting is allowing yourself to enjoy the materials. The main aim of this project is to see what they can do rather than what you can do. Try to relax and watch what happens with interest, rather than being too critical of yourself. You will need a large piece of paper and the paints, brushes and other mark-making tools you gathered earlier.

An exercise in mark-making
The project is to make as many kinds of marks as you can. With different tools you can make blobs, smears, draggings, squiggles, patches, anything. The painting on the opposite page shows a sponge print, lines straight from the tube, a line with a square-ended brush, a finger, a palette knife smear, a big brush stroke and stipple, and a toothbrush flick.

On your marks
The marks you make will sometimes accidentally look like "real" things. Some tools are good for creating leaves, others for cat's fur, clouds and so on. The marks in these examples look like foliage, grass and flowers. When you have filled a page with different marks, pick out the ones that remind you of real things and then make them part of a separate painting of your own, using appropriate colors.

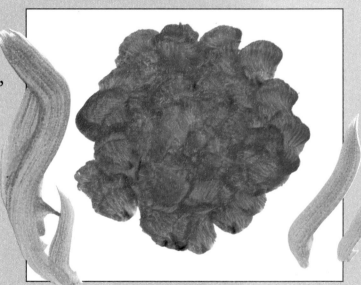

It also includes a trail, made by letting the paint run by picking the paper up and turning it, and two sable brush lines (the brush was turned to get both thick and thin lines). Can you tell which is which?

Slow or speedy?
The kind of paint used here is acrylic, but use whatever you have or try several kinds of paint together.

Don't try and make a "real" picture but spend time noticing the different effects you can produce. At this stage the marks don't "mean" anything, but you will notice that some look speedy and others slow. Some are soft, others look rough and crude. Notice how different tools, for example, a soft brush or a hard knife, make the paint behave in very different ways.

△ *"Above is a variety of marks I made using colors at random and as many different tools as I could find. After you have experimented with this, choose colors to suit particular kinds of marks, or try the whole project in one color."*

41

PURE COLOR

This project is to give you a chance to get to know the colors in your tubes or paintbox and to practice using them *flat*, in their pure form, without mixing them together.

If you look around you, you will see all kinds of colors, some bright, some dull, some easy to name, and some neither one nor the other. The world can look very complicated when you start trying to paint it. Some painters avoid looking at real things and just make things up! But most people like to paint what they see, at least from time to time.

Choosing your subject

Make a collection of everyday objects that correspond as closely as possible with the six pure colors from the color wheel (bottom right). Don't forget to include something to use as background – a bright curtain, perhaps, or a piece of colored paper. Find something red, blue, green, yellow, orange and purple. Take some time arranging everything in a group so that you can see all the objects clearly and they aren't in each other's way. Your painting will turn out very bright and cheerful.

You may like the bright colors so much that in future you may paint things brighter than they really are. Keep the colors clean when painting by using a different brush for each new color or by making sure you clean your brushes thoroughly between colors.

▽ *"For the painting below I first made a simple drawing in pencil. I spent some time deciding where the colors would go. You can see that some of the marks look a bit like the ones I made on the previous page. Paint several pictures of this subject and choose the one you like best."*

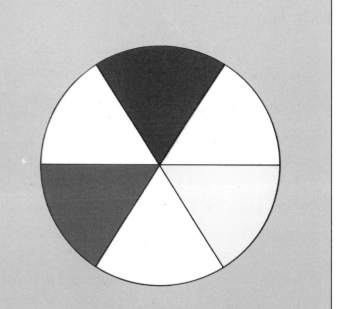

Primary colors

Here are the three basic or *primary* colors and their position on what is called the "color wheel." There are many kinds of red, yellow and blue but the primaries are the purest you can get.

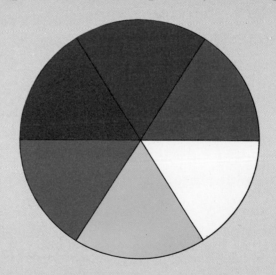

Secondary colors

Here are the primaries again with their neighbors: orange, green and purple. These are the *secondary* colors, mixed from the two primaries on either side of them. Experiment with painting the color wheel yourself.

43

MIXING COLORS

The pure colors used on the previous page can be put into pairs of opposites or *complementaries*. These are red and green, yellow and purple, and blue and orange. You can see them opposite each other on the color wheel. Black and white are also opposites and will be dealt with more fully below and on page 47. Some pictures are painted entirely with two complementaries, creating other colors by mixing them in different ways. Landscapes are often made of red and green, and these are the two colors used in the picture opposite, mixed with white in places.

Landscapes in pairs of colors

In the fall, when the sky is often clear and the leaves are bright, or in spring, with new life growing, other pairs of colors may be more appropriate. Winter could be seen as black and white. See if you can think of other subjects that would suit a particular pair of complementaries. Every color, however subtle, has its own complementary.

Paint a simple landscape in a pair of complementaries mixed with white. You may be surprised to discover that you don't need many colors to paint an interesting and atmospheric picture. Use different kinds of brushwork, thick and thin, fast and slow, for different effects.

Inside or out?

If you enjoy painting from life, go out looking for a subject or just paint the view from your window. On the other hand, you may prefer painting a place you know from memory, or just making something up. Whichever you choose, begin painting by mixing some colors on the palette, keeping them fresh and separate.

▷ *"In the painting on the right I have used pure color in the foreground (the part of the picture that looks nearest to the viewer), and mixes of red and green for the foliage and tree trunks beyond. For the sky, road and the grass in the distance I have added white. I made a pencil sketch first, then mixed my colors and began."*

White has the effect of making colors both lighter and less bright. With the exception of watercolors, all mediums use white to increase subtlety, but overuse can make your pictures look chalky and washed out. With watercolor, subtlety is obtained by using varying amounts of water to dilute the color. When you surround white with a pure color, it will appear to be tinged with the complementary of the pure color. Try it and see.

Pairs of opposites

Colors mixed with white become more subtle, as shown in the top left corner of each color square. When mixed together, complementary colors make grey, as shown in the bottom right corners. Painted side by side, opposite colors enhance or bring out the best in each other.

BRIGHTNESS, TONE AND HUE

Learning about colors is a bit like learning to speak a different language. If the first few pages of this chapter seem like hard work, think of them as needing to learn a new vocabulary so that you can express yourself with confidence in the future.

All colors have three qualities
These qualities are brightness, tone and hue. The brightness or dullness of a color compares with a loud or soft note in music. Tone means how light or dark a color is when compared to another color. A note in music has an equivalent high or low sound. Lastly, each color also has a hue, which is equivalent to the actual note in music. The hue is the actual color you are left with when

Playing scales in color
Brightness, tone and hue are illustrated in the color charts on the right. The top one demonstrates a progression of brightness to dullness, the middle shows light to dark tones, and the bottom one is a progression of the color pink to green in the same tone and brightness, to demonstrate hue. If colors of the same tone and brightness are placed side by side, as shown below, they seem to shimmer and dance together in front of your eyes. It is difficult to get this right, but if you learn to recognize when it *is* right you are beginning to get some real control with color-mixing.

46

differences in tone and brightness have been removed.

Seeing hue

The idea of this project is to make a picture in which all the colors are the same tone and as much as possible the same brightness. What you will then see is their hue. Choose some colors; experiment with mixing them and painting them in simple patches. The patches below have been made into buildings. First mix your colors. Look at them on the palette and change them around until they are all the same tone before you start painting. Use black to darken or quiet colors if they look too light or too bright. Try to keep the colors clean and flat.

◁ *"To keep colors on separate brushes clean, I stand the brushes bristles up in a can with holes punched in the lid. Alternatively, you could use a container filled with scrunched-up chicken wire."*

Black is introduced here as a way of making colors darker in tone and less bright. It can also be used as a color in its own right. Like white, it may appear to be affected by colors that surround it. Sometimes painters use lines of black to separate the colors in their pictures, as panes of colored glass are separated. This can have the effect of bringing order to a chaotic image.

47

MAKING IT LOOK "REAL"

Two painters once had a competition to see who could paint the most realistic picture. The pictures were to be unveiled to the judges. The first drew back the curtains. His picture was of fruit in a bowl. Birds came and pecked at it. Everyone was very impressed. The second painter was asked to draw back his curtains to reveal his picture. He replied that they were already looking at it. He had painted a pair of curtains.

Painting in 3-D
There is always a special kind of thrill in making something you paint look real. We all know the world is made up of solid things we can pick up or walk around. But the surface of a painting, board or piece of paper is flat. If you are painting an apple, how can you make it look fresh and good enough to eat?

One way to make your pictures look solid is to examine how light falls on the subject. As the sun moves across the sky and the shadows come and go, the appearance of your subject can change very much. The world changes constantly in front of you as you try to capture it, especially outside on a sunny day.

Careful observation
Find a simply colored object, an apple or an orange perhaps.

Look carefully at how its hues, tones and brightness change as you move it around. Look at it closely, get to know the apple in all lights, and familiarize yourself with its shape and colors. Try placing the apple so that the light comes strongly from one direction. Paint the apple in your mind's eye before you begin. Then make three paintings, each showing a different effect of light.

▽ *"My examples below show the same apple in three different lights. Notice how my colors become gradually darker and bluer as the shadows deepen. Make your picture life-size or larger, so you can really show what's happening without getting bogged down in small details."*

Changing light
The diagrams below show the effects of light shined on a round form from a number of different directions (indicated by the arrows). Reproducing this effect will involve the technique of blending colors. As the light changes to shadow, so colors change accordingly. You might practice these changes on a separate piece of paper before beginning your painting. Some painters feel that the shadow of an object can be represented by the complementary of the color that is in the light. Do your observations bear this out?

PORTRAITS

"Why can't you be more like an apple!" Cezanne used to shout at people he was painting. A head may be a bit like an apple but a face has expressions and doesn't find it easy to stay still and always look the same.

Beginning work
The project here is to paint a portrait. Ask someone to pose for you who won't mind whether your picture is like them or not. Grandparents can be ideal. Make sure that your subject is comfortable and relaxed. Alternatively, paint with a friend, working on one another's portraits.

Step by step
Take time to have a good look at your subject. Then begin by drawing in pencil, and then with very thin paint, the simple shape of the face. Mark in the lines for the features as shown in the diagram below. Lightly lay in the eyes, ears, nose, mouth and hair. Have a good look at the color of your model's skin, hair and clothes, and the color of the background.

Setting the mood
Mix up the main colors you need. Remember that they, as much as anything else, will give the picture its mood. Adjust them until you are satisfied with your basic ingredients. Then paint them down as flat areas of color. Give your portrait depth and solidity by modeling highlights and shadows over the flat colors.

▷ *"My examples show the four stages described above. Light is shining on the face from one side, and I have introduced light and shadow areas accordingly. Don't be afraid of changing your picture as you go along. The character of your subject may only become clear gradually. It's important not to put in too many details at an early stage, for you may be reluctant to paint over them even if you should."*

Proportions of the head
The drawing near right shows the average proportions of the head. One thing that may surprise you is that the eyes come halfway down the head and not higher up, as you might suppose. The lower part is divided in half again where the nose ends, and in half again at the mouth. The second picture shows the proportions of the same head in *profile*, from a side view.

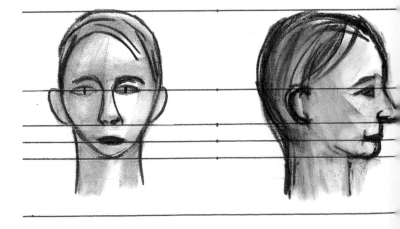

MOOD AND FEELING

This page is all about expressing feeling with paint. Imagine that you meet with an alien from outer space on a visit to Earth. This creature comes from a scientifically advanced planet whose inhabitants are incapable of experiencing emotion. Your paintings must convey these unknown things to him/her/it.

Making the unseen visible

Painting, like music, has the power to communicate happiness, sadness, calm, rage. If you are human rather than alien, paintings will also stir emotions inside you as music does. The project here is about expressing moods and feelings in paint. Decide what emotion you want to try first; it will help if you get in the mood yourself, perhaps by playing some appropriate music.

Be a conductor of energy

Let the emotion you have chosen wash over you. What colors and shapes come to mind? There isn't a right and wrong way of doing this, though some find it easier than others. When you have finished, try a different emotion, sadness or boredom perhaps – if you ever say you feel bored, now is the time to paint the most boring picture you can!

▷ *"My paintings show two contrasting sets of emotions. Here are some pairs of adjectives you might like to try: angry and calm; relaxed and uncomfortable; friendly and hostile; extravagant and stingy. Dream up other pairs yourself."*

△ Happiness
▽ Excitement

△ Misery

▽ Peacefulness

Mood, shape and color

There are no strict rules linking colors with particular feelings. Blue is usually thought of as sad but it can also be peaceful; orange can be cheerful but also angry. Yellow can be warm like the sun, but quite the opposite as the color of someone's face. It all depends on how color is used.

Shape can also express mood and emotion. A triangle sits firmly on the ground and might convey stability, or hope. A rectangle may also seem calm, or it might feel restrictive. A circle seems likely to move or float; it might convey a sense of completeness or of isolation. A star explodes with vitality, and seems to grow bigger as you look at it. Which colors fit best with each of these shapes?

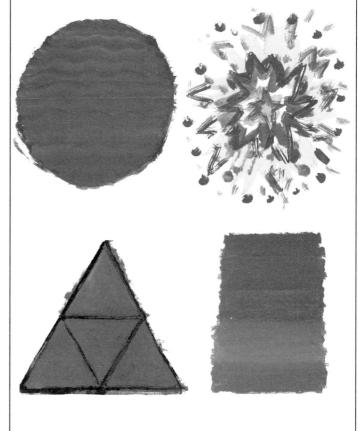

EXPRESSING YOURSELF

Painters paint self-portraits for all kinds of reasons, but the most obvious has to be that your own face is always there when you want it. Have a good look in the mirror and see what shape yours is. Ask yourself what kind of person you are and how you can show this in a painting. Are you cheerful or sad? Do you shout a lot or do you keep things bottled up? Do you like to do things quickly, or do you take your time? Using some of the ideas from the previous projects, try to combine careful observation and the expression of feeling in a portrait of yourself.

Getting set up
Begin by getting comfortable. Place your paper or board on an easel or rest it against a wall or the back of a chair. Arrange yourself in such a way that you can look straight from the mirror to your painting without turning your head too much.

Make a pencil sketch as you did earlier, taking care to establish the particular proportions of your face. Mix your colors, and change them around until you are satisfied that they represent you.

Showing how you feel
Do several pictures of yourself in different moods and change the colors and the way you put on the paint accordingly. After the first painting, you may want to dispense with the mirror and paint your "inner self" from imagination.

△ "These three portraits use color to convey mood. This boy in shades of pink looks gentle and thoughtful."

Features and expressions
Here are examples of the same face with three very different expressions, looking in turn angry, frightened and perplexed. These emotions are conveyed chiefly through the shape of the mouth and eyes. Notice, however, that the eyebrows, hair, even the nose and ears can also express emotion. Lines and shapes turning upward look cheerful and full of life; turning down they look sad or fierce. To convey perplexity the lines are undecided and may turn in both directions.

△ "I have tried to convey the scattiness and good humor of this boy through the use of bright colors and jagged strokes."

△ "My third sitter seemed anxious and sad. I chose gloomy colors and applied them with nervous, scratchy strokes."

IMAGINATION

Imagination means image-making. With it you can create pictures of things that in real life could never happen (or not very often anyway). Through painting you can create a world which is strange, magical, shocking or just plain crazy.

Unusual combinations

The project here is to base a painting on the idea of combining two unrelated subjects. When these come together they make something new with a separate life of its own. The illustration near right shows a man and a tree. In the painting opposite, the same words came together to make a tree-man. If you look in the background you will see a man-tree as an alternative.

Seeing pictures in your head

One way of getting ideas for a painting of this kind is to write down lots of ideas on separate pieces of paper and put them in a bag.

Pick pairs of them at random out of the bag. When you see two words together, what picture, if any, comes into your mind of how they could be joined? Keep trying different combinations. Practice seeing as much detail as possible in your mind's eye before starting to paint.

▷ *"My tree-man picture is painted with a big brush for the trees and sky and a smaller one for the head and hands. The brush marks in the foreground and in the foliage look like grass and leaves."*

Changing step by step

The idea of putting together two things and making a third can be a starting point for all kinds of ideas. Opposite you can see how a man changing into a tiger might work step by step. This process is called transformation or metamorphosis. Perhaps you can imagine how a similar sequence happened while the man was changing into a tree, which the main picture shows halfway through. How would it look at an earlier or later stage in the process of transformation?

There are many other ways of using your imagination. Dreams provide images that can become powerful paintings – can you remember any of yours? Daydreaming can also make amazing and wonderful things come true. A wolf hatching from an egg? A fossilized car?

COMPOSITION

As discussed previously on page 22, composition literally means putting things together. If you take the ingredients for a cake and taste them separately, it is not the same as tasting the cake itself. In the same way your picture is made up of different ingredients that come together to form a new whole. Within it, colored shapes and light and dark areas have to work together. Each part must be in place and not demand your attention so much that you can't see the picture as a single thing.

Try it yourself
A good way to practice composition is by using colored paper which can be cut or torn to the shape you want. By moving your pieces of paper around, you can experiment to achieve a sense of unity before you finally glue them down.

Ripping off ideas
A good subject for this technique, called collage, is people in action. Look through newspapers or magazines to find a photograph that appeals to you for your subject. Then compose your own collage based loosely on the photograph. Don't glue anything down until you have tried your ingredients in a number of different positions first.

▷ *"My composition is basically triangular. Your eyes climb up to the ball as the soccer players do. Some of the colored pieces for the arms and legs don't look very real on their own, but they play their part in the whole."*

A journey around your picture
Compositions are often based on simple shapes like a triangle, a circle or a spiral. Having first seen the whole image, your eyes then follow the movement of the composition. In the team picture your eyes can either look along the rows of heads or move in a zigzag between them. What happens when you look at the runners below? Always try to give your eyes an exciting journey.

PERSPECTIVE

Perspective, which means "looking through," is a way of creating the illusion of three-dimensional space on the flat surface of a picture. The kind of perspective that is usually most familiar is based on the idea that the painting on the wall is like a window through which we can see the real world.

Getting angles right

Everyone knows how difficult it can sometimes be to get a particular angle of a building or table exactly right, so that it looks as if it were moving toward or away from us. People who find this skill difficult to master often give up the idea of being good at art before they have discovered all the

Background   Middle ground   Foreground

other aspects of painting that are exciting and enjoyable.

Creating distance

There are at least four different ways of showing that one thing is behind or in front of another. Many pictures combine several or all four, though some use none at all.

◁ *"The sky in my picture opposite shows that a strong blue can appear to be in front of a paler, thinner blue as it fades toward the horizon. I used the brightest colors in the foreground and middle distance. I applied the paint thickly and more vigorously in those areas too."*

For the painter perhaps the most appropriate way of portraying distance is through color. As a rule, dark and dull colors tend to go back, or recede, in space. Light and bright ones tend to come forward. Think of how the rays of a yellow sun reach out from a background of blue sky.

The strongest contrasts in tone should be in the foreground. Colors in a landscape seem to get bluer and mistier the further away they are, and the same effect can be achieved in painting. Recession can also be emphasized by using thinner paint in the middle and background. Paint a landscape and test out these theories.

A sense of space

The diagrams below illustrate some of the other ways of showing perspective. The first is an example of "linear" or line perspective. Lines that would in fact run parallel in the real world, like the roadsides in the diagram, appear to meet at a point on the horizon called the "vanishing point."

The second diagram shows an example of overlapping. The hill that blocks out part of another hill must be in front of it; the human figure blocks them all out and so must be the nearest thing to you. In the third diagram the darker, stronger and "speedier" lines and tones in the foreground appear to be in front of the softer, "slower" lines.

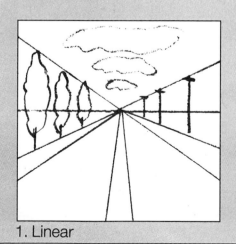

1. Linear

2. Overlapping

3. Tonal

DIFFERENT WAYS OF SEEING

Long ago ancient civilizations had very different ways of viewing the world than we in the West are familiar with today. Persian, Indian, Egyptian and Chinese cultures all evolved artistic traditions that reflected their own outlooks. For some of them the idea was not to show what a scene looked like from any one place or at one time, but to represent their subject from a number of viewpoints at once, or at a number of different times simultaneously.

Seeing the world as flat

Many modern painters have placed a similar importance on the picture as a flat pattern in which every part is of equal value. In their work, colors and shapes sit side by side on the surface of the picture, as they do in the main painting below, rather than trying to fool the eye and create the illusion of space, as shown in the watercolor below left.

Seeing from many angles

Try this approach with a painting of your own room at home. This project is not about standing on one spot, gazing ahead and painting what you see with mathematical precision. Walk around your room instead and decide which viewpoint is best for each of the objects you want to include. You could also put yourself in the picture.

▽ *"Below is a room I have painted from a single viewpoint with linear perspective. The space in the room is defined by receding lines which make the front look bigger and the rear smaller."*

▷ *"My painting on the right involves a number of different viewpoints. The table-top is seen from above, the vase from the side, while the fruit bowl is a bit of both."*

Through Egyptian eyes

A striking example of multiviewpoint is found in the art of the ancient Egyptians, whose style of painting remained almost unchanged for 5,000 years. Egyptian tradition demanded the representation of certain things from particular angles, regardless of whether it was possible to see these angles simultaneously in the real world. Artists felt that this method would best express the essence of their subject. A face, for example, should be shown from the side, whereas an eye was most like an eye when seen from the front. This method produced an idealization rather than a copy of the world.

PRESENTATION

Your work will always look better when it is put into a mat or a frame and hung on a wall. Pictures need to be separated from everyday life to be seen properly. Looking over your work over a period of time will also help you to see it as a separate thing.

Reworking
You may notice things you want to change. Sometimes you may find that there are parts that you don't like: for example, a color may appear too bright or too dull. Reworking should be approached with caution. If your picture is free and spontaneous, you may spoil it by overpainting.

When to stop
Judging the right moment to stop is an important skill to develop. When that decision is made, the painting has reached the end of its journey and must be able to stand by itself.

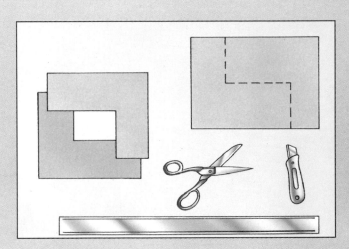

Selecting your image
If your painting does not seem to work satisfactorily as it is, part of it may. Selecting which part to use can be fascinating. By cutting out a pair of L-shapes as shown in the diagram above, you can isolate a portion that may look more appealing on its own. By moving the L-shapes over the surface of the picture, you can change the size and shape of your composition very easily. Then by measuring the space within the L-shapes you can find out the dimensions for your mat.

Mounting your work
When you have decided on your final composition, cut a mat to display it. Mats should be cut equally on both sides, but make sure your mat is wider at the bottom than at the top, as shown in the middle mat below. Otherwise when it is hanging the mat will look unbalanced.

A pale gray or cream mat is right for many pictures, but sometimes colored mats can be effective. Choose a color that brings out the mood or the colors of the picture. On the whole, avoid very brightly colored mats, as they will tend to draw attention away from your actual painting.

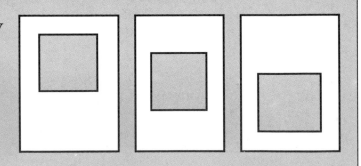

PRACTICAL TIPS ON PAINTING

Your starting kit

Before you begin painting, you will need a starting kit of basic equipment. Whichever **paint** you choose, you will need at least five colors – start with cadmium red, cadmium yellow, ultramarine (blue), white and black. Add yellow ochre, viridian (green), burnt umber and cobalt blue if you can.

Many kinds of **brushes** are available, suitable for different kinds of paint. Brushes are numbered according to size. You will need at least three brushes to begin with: a thick and a thin coarse brush, and a fine brush for details. Brush prices vary greatly; more expensive ones will probably last longer and produce better results.

A **palette knife** can be used to apply oil or acrylic paint, to produce hard, flat marks or to build up layers of paint. For a **palette** you could use an old plate (a white one is best) or tin lid. For water-soluble paints you will need jelly jars to hold water and for oil or acrylic paint a **dipper** or some small containers for your thinners (discussed below).

Preparing your surface

Before you use oil or acrylic paint you will need to *prime* your surface, unless you are using a prepared canvas. For acrylic paint use a special acrylic primer. For oil paint, give your surface a coat of primer such as size or gesso, using a household paint brush.

Stretching your paper will be necessary if you use water-soluble paint. Immerse your paper in water so that both sides are thoroughly wet.

Place it on a flat board, and smooth out the creases with a sponge. Tape it to the board with brown paper tape, and let it dry. Leave your paper taped to the board while you paint. Later, if you remove the tape with your finished painting, it will fit well under a mat.

Adding thinners

Paint is usually *thinned*, or diluted, but the thinner that should be used varies with the kind of paint. Water-soluble paints like watercolors, gouache, powder and poster paint are diluted with water. Oil paint is thinned with linseed oil and turpentine.

Acrylic paint can be diluted with various liquids, or *media*, to give different effects. It can be thinned with water, but you can also buy a medium to slow down the drying time of the paint. Other media create a gloss or matte effect.

Cleaning up

After using water-soluble paints (including acrylic), brushes should be rinsed in water immediately. Smooth the hairs of your brushes back into shape and stand them bristles up to dry.

After using oils, brushes should be wiped on a rag or newspaper to remove excess paint. They should be cleaned first with turpentine and then with soap and water.

Put your oil painting somewhere safe to dry, which may take several months. When it is dry, you can paint it with a coat of varnish to protect it and give it a glossy surface.

Cartooning is about having fun and developing a new skill at the same time. If you are the sort of person who sees the funny side of things, now is the chance to get some of your ideas down on paper. And if you've always wanted to have adventures, now you can invent strip cartoons in which anything can happen.

This chapter introduces you to different kinds of cartoons and to the wide range of materials you can use for cartooning. You don't need to be great at drawing; many cartoons are based on a few simple lines.

The first cartoons

Originally a cartoon was a sketch made in preparation for a more finished work – an outline for a painting, tapestry, or mosaic. The cartoons made by the Italian artist Leonardo da Vinci in the fifteenth century are still famous today. Today, a cartoon is a particular kind of drawing, direct and effective, often funny. The best cartoons often say something about life that everyone knows deep down to be true, but is afraid to own up to! A sequence of cartoons may be used to tell a story – a comic strip – or they can be used to make a cartoon film.

▷ *"These four cartoons are of characters who just emerged when I started doodling. There's no limit to the number and variety of types waiting to jump out of your head too. The one at the top right thinks he is drawing something very funny – I hope this happens to you!"*

JOKES AND CARICATURES

Over the next pages you can see the different types of cartoon and the materials they can be drawn with.

Visual jokes

The simplest cartoon of all is a picture which makes a joke. The drawing itself can also be funny, or can surprise us. Alternatively, it's the cartoon character who's about to get a surprise; we can see it coming but the character can't!

Some cartoon jokes are effective without words; others rely on a worded caption to make the point. If more than one character is speaking, speech bubbles will be needed.

Pencil and felt-tip pen

The most basic tools for cartooning are pencils and felt-tips. A soft pencil produces a friendly line (below left). You can go over a sketch in pencil with felt-tip or ink, and then rub out mistakes with an eraser.

Felt-tips come in different thicknesses. A fine pen makes an elegant line (center) and a thick or chiseled marker (right) produces strong, solid marks.

Many kinds of paper are suitable for cartooning. Newsprint paper is inexpensive. Thin paper like tracing paper is useful for tracing and redoing images if you make a mistake.

Caricature

A caricature is a drawing of a real person in which individual features, like the size of the person's nose, or the shape of the chin, are exaggerated. Yet, somehow a likeness is achieved. In fact, if cleverly done, a caricature can look more like the individual than he or she does in real life! Some people, unfortunately for them, are easier to caricature than others.

This style of cartooning has a long history. For thousands of years cartoonists have been making caricatures of public figures. They can be kind or cruel, flattering or grotesque, depending on the artist.

Ink, charcoal and conté

Pen and ink, charcoal and conté are all lively materials suitable for caricaturing different kinds of people. Ink can be used with a dip-pen or a fountain pen, and with nibs of different sizes. Ink makes free, expressive lines (left below).

Charcoal gives a dark line for dramatic portraits (middle below). It can produce a rough and ready look, or can be smudged with your finger to make velvety shadows.

Conté comes in shades of brown or gray. It produces soft, warm marks good for caricatures like the hairy, bearlike person below right.

CARTOON STRIPS AND ANIMATION

Cartoon strips

Cartoon strips are a sequence of individual cartoons that tell a story. From cave paintings to the Bayeux tapestry, from Mickey Mouse to Garfield, the principle is to show developing action through a series of images. Have a look through some of your own cartoon books to see the vast range of styles that can be used.

We often enjoy strip cartoons without noticing the techniques artists use to show closeup or long distance views, to indicate drama, tension, or a change of pace. Filmmakers and animators use similar techniques to produce the same kinds of effects.

Cartooning in color

Cartoon strips are usually in color. Many color materials are available. Colored pencils are easy to use. You can create pale and dark tones by pressing lightly or heavily, and new colors by laying one color over another (left). Watercolor and gouache (middle picture) are both good for cartooning. Watercolor is washed on thinly and is transparent. Gouache is denser and opaque. For both you will need to use thick paper, as thin paper will wrinkle up.

Felt-tips (right) are also versatile. Chunky, wedge-shaped ones cover the paper quickly and evenly; thin ones are good for outlines.

Animation

Animation is a way of bringing pictures to life by making them appear to move. When we watch a modern cartoon film, we seem to see a smooth sequence of movement. It's hard to believe we are actually looking at thousands of single pictures, each one slightly different from the last. They change in front of our eyes so quickly we can't see when one image replaces another.

Later in the book we will look at the techniques animators use. You can practice some of these tricks yourself. If you enjoy being precise and working carefully, you can get some very impressive results.

Painting on acetate

For the purposes of animation, cartoons are painted on sheets of clear plastic called acetate. Both sides of the acetate are used, as shown below. The image is drawn on one side with a special oil-based pen called an o.h.p. (overhead projector pen). The image is colored in on the other side using gouache or acrylic paint. This may be done quite messily, because when the acetate is turned over again, the brush marks will be invisible. Small pads of acetate are available and can be bought in art stores. Try cartooning on acctate yourself; the result will look very effective positioned on a window with light shining through it.

BASICS: HEADS GALORE

All styles of cartooning rely on a few basic ideas. Let's look at them first in terms of cartooning heads.

Faces are everywhere if you know how to look, in trees and clouds, even in clothes hanging on the door knob at night. For the cartoonist, using the imagination is very important.

Eggheads

A cartoon head usually starts life as a balloon or egg shape. The basic ingredients of a face are two dots for eyes, an L-shape for a nose and a line for the mouth. But the way you combine these basic ingredients can suggest all kinds of characters (see the faces below left).

Begin your cartooning career by doing variations on this theme. Then experiment with different shapes, choosing a particular shape for the head and echoing the same shape as you draw in the features.

Positioning the features

Eyes set far apart look confident; eyes set close together (bottom right) look silly, or shy. Features placed at the bottom of the head look clever; features placed at the top look self-satisfied.

Shapes and personalities

The shape of the head suggests personality; draw features to match. A pear-shaped face looks sad, a square head looks mechanical. A curvy face looks flabby and a star-shape is full of energy.

72

▷ *"Once you start drawing, ideas will come. I didn't plan the character shown right, but added details as I went along, as if I were making up an actress for a role."*

Faces step by step

Try building your own cartoon personalities. Start with a basic head shape and gradually add features, hair and clothes. Then draw your character again, with a different expression this time.

▽ *"Expressions affect not only the mouth but all the features, the shape of the face, even the hair. Try some expressions yourself in front of the mirror. Cartoon expressions are even more pronounced."*

73

BASICS: GETTING THINGS MOVING

Action in cartoons needs to be shown as simply and clearly as possible. The secret of drawing cartoon figures on the move is to start with a few simple lines and build up from there.

The skeleton is the basis of all figures, human or animal; that's where stick people come in. The stick figure represents the skeleton and is an ideal way of practicing positions and movements. Try a series of stick figures before you commit yourself to a more developed drawing.

▷ *"Action can often be summed up by a single line. One way to get your imagination moving is to sketch a line at random and see what it can be turned into! The examples on the right show lines of movement evolving into finished cartoons. Notice how movement can be emphasized by the addition of speed lines and small details like the flying pipe and hat."*

▽ *"Fill pages of your sketch book with stick people running, jumping, somersaulting, doing everything under the sun! When you're happy with your action people, start to flesh them out into sausage figures, as shown below."*

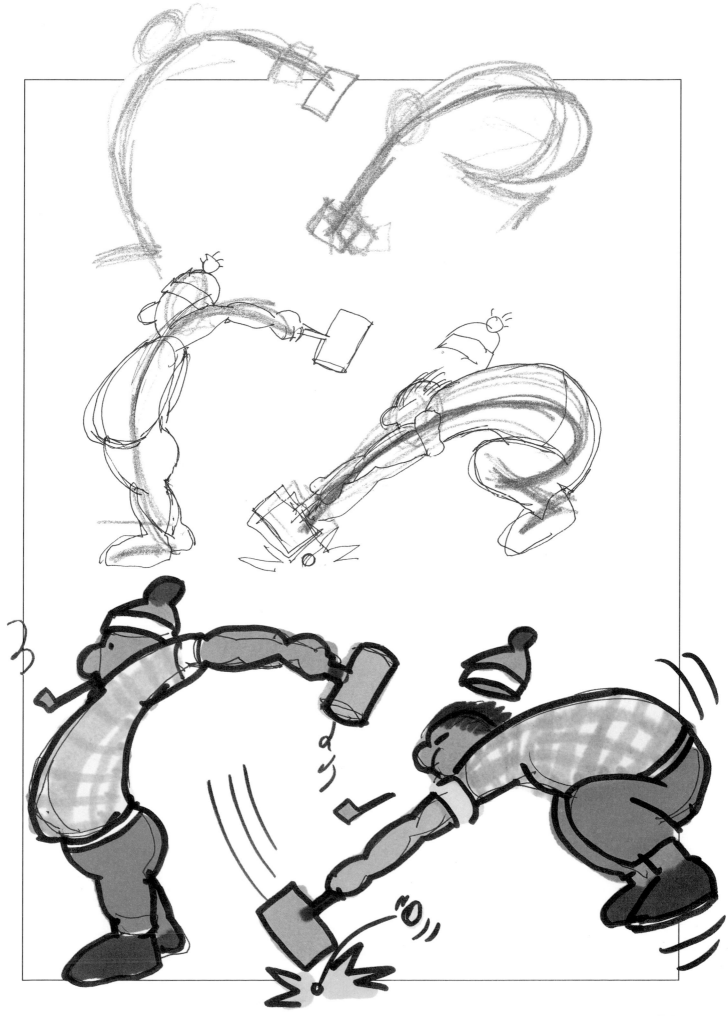

BASICS: POINTS OF VIEW

"Everybody's got to be somewhere," as a comedian once said. Where are you now? Everyone reading this will give a different answer. In cartoons the action can be set anywhere from the bottom of the sea to the inside of a shoe. Sometimes the best jokes have more to do with the setting than what the characters are doing or saying.

How things change size

Cartoon backgrounds are usually kept simple. But in cartoons, as in real life, things look bigger the closer they are to you, and things look small if they are far away. This is called perspective, and in cartoons the effect is often even more exaggerated. Look at the girl on the railroad track (bottom left below). The train is really bigger than she is but it seems smaller because it's further away.

Looking up and down

Perspective affects how things appear from different angles, as you can see from the cartoons on the right. The same knight looks very different from various angles: straight on, from below and above. Parts of his body loom large, or dwindle away, depending on how close they are to us. It takes a bit of practice to get this looking right, and it may help to work from stick and sausage men, as you did on the previous page.

▷ *"Different angles increase the drama and impact of your cartooning. The face-on view is the least dramatic. Seen from below looking up (not a good idea in this instance) the knight's feet and fists look huge. Viewed from above, his helmet and sword seem to zoom toward us as he sweeps past."*

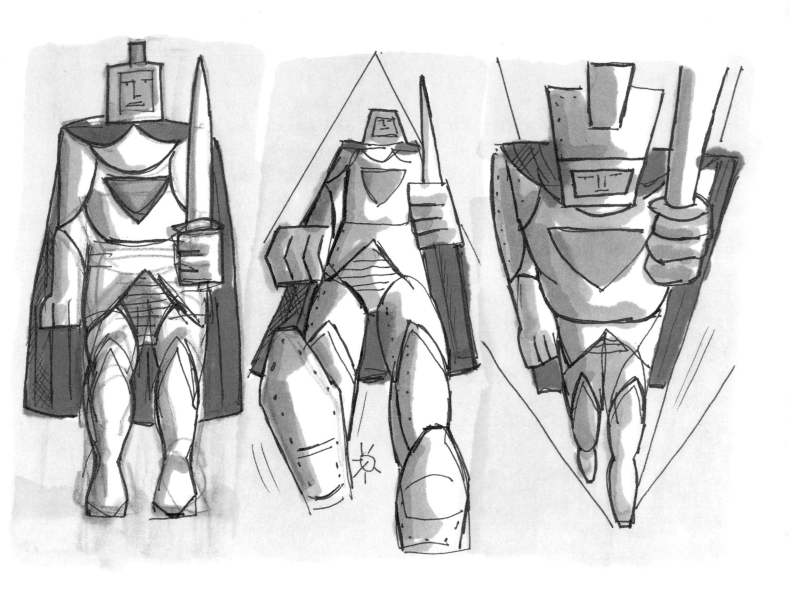

Tiny or tremendous?

Background makes all the difference to how we understand, or "read," a cartoon. The top two cartoons on the left show how the same girl seems to change size, depending on the background she is seen against. Playing with scale is fun and there are lots of tricks you can try. Practice putting your own character in different settings.

Putting things in perspective

The girl on the railroad track is an example of a kind of perspective called linear, or line, perspective.

The lines of the railroad track run parallel. But they appear to converge at the vanishing point. All parallel obey this rule of perspective. Sketching lines in pencil fanning in toward that vanishing point (see drawings above) can help get things in perspective.

Perspective can also be shown by a technique called overlapping. The girl overlaps and conceals some of the houses (bottom right) and so seems to be standing in front of them. The car overlaps the sidewalk and so looks the closest of all.

CARTOON PUNS

At its simplest a cartoon is something that makes us laugh. What kinds of things do *you* find funny? It's a great feeling when something you thought of makes other people laugh too. On this page we will look at the most basic jokes of all, those without words or captions, and explore how you can dream them up for yourself.

Visual puns

Many jokes without words rely on visual puns. A visual pun is a joke based on a shape with two meanings, just as a verbal pun is based on a word with two meanings. The cartoon at the top on the opposite page is an example of a visual pun.

Doodle power

Develop your ability to find visual puns by doodling. Draw a simple shape, like the rectangle, coil and zig-zag patterns shown in red below. Or draw some random squiggles with a friend and then swap over. Have a good look at the lines and see what they suggest to you. Turn the paper around and look at it from all sides. Your squiggle could be anything – it's a question of allowing your imagination to run wild.

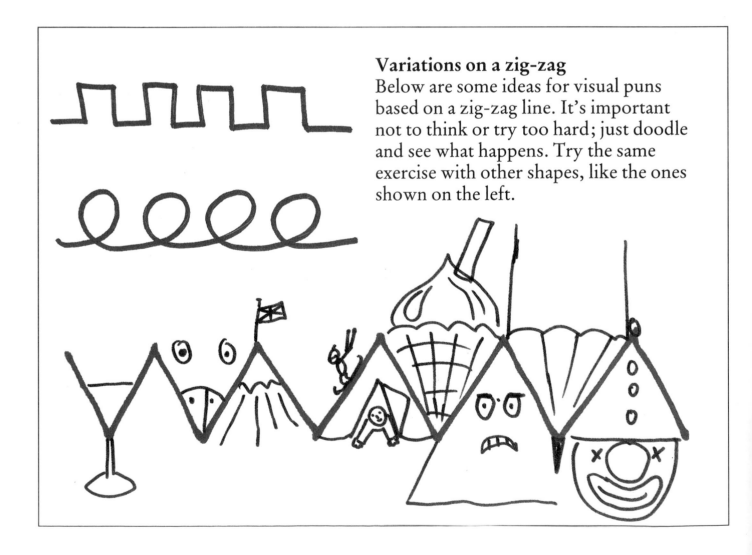

Variations on a zig-zag

Below are some ideas for visual puns based on a zig-zag line. It's important not to think or try too hard; just doodle and see what happens. Try the same exercise with other shapes, like the ones shown on the left.

Doing two jobs

Another type of joke without words is about an object with two functions. The blindfold is common to both pictures below, but in the second it is put to an unexpected use. What other everyday objects can you think of that could have more than one use? Let your imagination loose on objects like umbrellas, baby carriages, aerosol sprays and walking sticks.

▷ *"This visual pun is drawn from the doodle on the previous page. The humor in many cartoons is based on anticipation: something is about to happen, but the character involved is not aware of it – yet!"*

Getting your point across

The joke here is about the blindfold, so it has been colored black to make it obvious. All the details in the first picture – the guns, the expressions of soldiers and prisoner – lead us to expect the worst. In the second picture the details reappear but are changed, emphasizing the contrast in mood.

I SUPPOSE YOU FIND THAT FUNNY

Some people think cartoons without words are the best. But whether in the form of speech bubbles, captions or signs, words add a whole new range of possibilities. Thinking up jokes is easier for some of us than for others. Exercises with words encourage jokes to spring to mind.

The punch line game

In cartoon jokes the point is often put across in the caption below the picture, called the punch line. An exercise you can try involves a simple punch line like "I suppose you find that funny." The exercise is to think of as many ways as possible to illustrate it. At least two people are implied, one of whom is not amused by the antics of the other. But what is happening, exactly?

There are other punch lines you could try with this. Possibilities include "Don't look now, but...," "I thought you said there were no side effects," or even "We can't go on meeting like this." Sketch rough ideas and develop one or two.

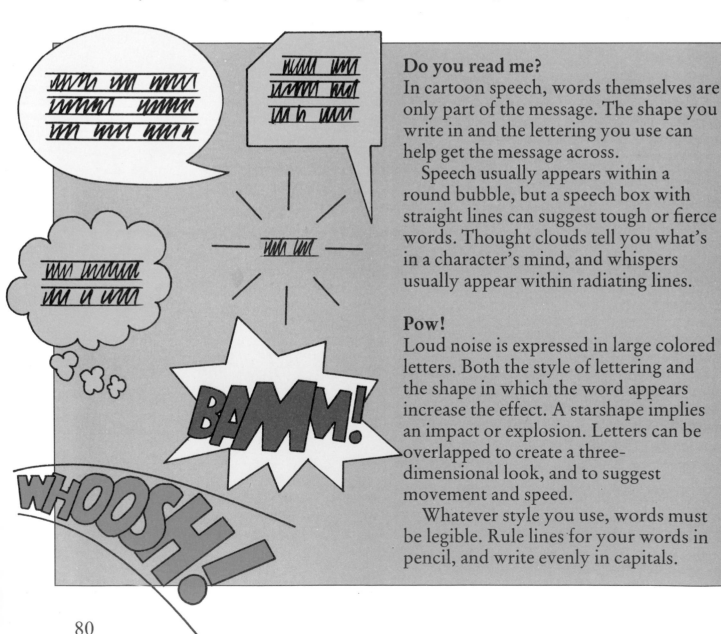

Do you read me?

In cartoon speech, words themselves are only part of the message. The shape you write in and the lettering you use can help get the message across.

Speech usually appears within a round bubble, but a speech box with straight lines can suggest tough or fierce words. Thought clouds tell you what's in a character's mind, and whispers usually appear within radiating lines.

Pow!

Loud noise is expressed in large colored letters. Both the style of lettering and the shape in which the word appears increase the effect. A starshape implies an impact or explosion. Letters can be overlapped to create a three-dimensional look, and to suggest movement and speed.

Whatever style you use, words must be legible. Rule lines for your words in pencil, and write evenly in capitals.

Lost in the jungle or all at sea?
Cartoonists often return to classic comic situations like hospitals, prisons, or car accidents. Why are these situations funny? They are often dangerous, embarrassing or unexpected – situations we'd rather not be in ourselves!

The joke is usually about how ordinary people react to extraordinary circumstances. Someone carried off by a monster might, for example, worry about whether they locked the back door. Funny things happen in everyday life too. Jot down ideas in a notebook for later use.

Shipwrecked? Stranded on the moon?
Below are two of the most common dilemmas cartoon characters find themselves in. Practice the punch line game in reverse by thinking up as many punch lines as possible for these two images. Bear in mind all the possible interpretations of the pictures.

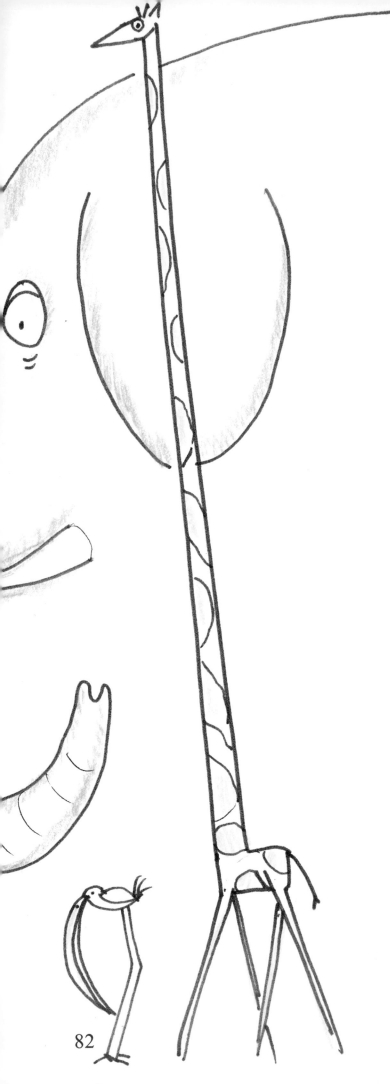

CARICATURE

Have you got a nickname? If you haven't, your teacher probably has. Nicknames are a bit like shorthand; we use them to sum people up, not always very kindly. If they stick, it's usually because they pinpoint something about that person's appearance or personality.

Caricatures are visual nicknames. Like nicknames, they focus on certain key characteristics and emphasize them. Like other kinds of cartoons, they are about simplifying and exaggerating what you see.

Animal crackers

Some caricaturists say that it helps them to think of a person as a particular animal. When we draw animals from imagination, we tend to focus on their most obvious features and emphasize them. A grizzly bear is all shaggy hair; a rhino is built like a tank, with stumpy legs and a giant horn. A monkey is thin and gangling, with rubbery legs and tail. Try caricaturing animals yourself from imagination or from photographs. Try doing a realistic drawing of each animal first, and then exaggerate it into a caricature.

◁ *"The main thing about an elephant is size. To emphasize this I've made mine so big it can't fit on the page, but I've left enough clues to identify it. Of course, the first thing you notice about a giraffe is the long neck. Wading birds have long legs and curved beaks for picking things off the bottom of the river bed, so these are the things I've chosen to exaggerate."*

Stretching a point

The same idea holds true of caricaturing both people and animals. Whether you choose your "victim" from real life or from photographs, you will need to get to know their face well. Study the face and decide which features – eyes, chin, hair, whatever – are most important. Make these stand out even more.

Not just heads

What you choose to emphasize is up to you. Two cartoonists will produce very different caricatures of the same person. And remember that caricatures can be about bodies, too. The size of chest or stomach, the length of arms and legs, the posture, whether slouched or upright, can all help your caricature work.

What's in a face?

In caricature the trick is to sum up and exaggerate. The first caricature below has focussed on the boy's frizzy hair and cheeky grin; the second (top right) has made the most of the eyeglasses, pointed nose and glum mouth of its subject. The studious girl gets messier hair, a snub nose and a more fixed expression, and the young man (bottom right) has an even haughtier look.

DO-IT-YOURSELF CARICATURE

Now that you know how caricature works, it's time to try some of your own. The first step is to choose your subject. It's good to pick someone you know well, and who you can observe from day to day. But you could try doing a caricature of a famous person you admire, or even one whom you dislike!

That's typical!
Before you begin drawing, you may have to do a bit of creative thinking.

Consider what pose, and what habits are most typical of your subject. Capturing the essence of someone's personality need not involve drawing their face or even much of their body at all. If Grandad spends most of his time in an armchair reading the newspaper, you could draw the newspaper with two hands holding it open and just the top of his head surrounded by the chair. Add smoke from a pipe and his old red slippers and it couldn't be anyone else.

The right tool for the job
Make sure the drawing materials you choose match your subject. Remember that pencils, pen and ink, charcoal, and conté all have a very different "feel."

Charcoal (below left) has a rich, soft look. Pen and ink has a spontaneous quality. The caricature on the right uses an ink wash to create shadows and a depressed, seedy look.

Clothes always help to identify your subject. Some people's hats and coats are so particular to them that a back view may be enough. Some people like to hide behind their accessories – look at the charcoal portrait far left on the opposite page.

▽ **"Caricatures of famous people can be fun: I chose John Wayne (below). First I did a drawing from a photograph to familiarize myself with my subject. I noted a square chin, the lift of one eyebrow. From movies I remembered a habit of talking out of one side of his mouth. As John Wayne is best known for cowboy parts, I added a hat, kerchief and checked shirt."**

85

CREATING A SUPERHERO

A cartoon strip is a series of pictures that tell a story, from the adventures of mischievous school friends to the exploits of fantasy superheroes. The next two pages are about creating your own cartoon strip, and the first step is to invent the characters.

What do Superman, the Incredible Hulk and the Teenage Mutant Ninja Turtles have in common? Most superheroes are concocted from a recipe of certain ingredients. Looking at these ingredients can help you build your own characters.

Factor X

Some superheroes come from other planets but most are from Earth; they are ordinary people (or animals) who have acquired a special ability, often as a result of some extraordinary event. This is sometimes linked to radiation, but not always; Popeye gets his great strength from an ordinary can of spinach.

A superhero has his or her own territory, a particular location to patrol. Cities are popular, and, of course, the far reaches of outer space.

Missions and superskills

All superheroes have a cause – to fight villains like the one shown above left, or to right a particular injustice in the world. Your superhero will need a mission and a special ability – think about the superpower you would most like to have for yourself!

A superpower can be extra strength, vision, or hearing, or it can be something new, from X ray vision to the ability to change shape. A superhero associated with an animal takes on the creature's powers – so the owl girl above might be able to see in the dark. Other favorite crime-fighters are themselves animals.

Developing a script

Your superhero can be developed by thinking about costume, weaknesses, likes and dislikes, sidekicks and friends. But the best way of learning about your superhero is to set out on an adventure and see how he or she does!

What makes a good storyline? Cartoon scripts often contain certain key ingredients. The strip begins with a problem: a crime or mystery which is often the work of a villain. It may be almost too late before the hero learns of the trouble and decides to step in.

Meanwhile, problems may mount up, and friends may be captured or wounded. In the nick of time comes a moment of inspiration, and the tide turns. Triumph! There is often a celebration before the hero heads home. Develop your plot along these lines and your superhero is ready to go!

▷ *"My superhero, Cartoonman, is a cool customer; here you can see him studying his script, unconcerned by the battle raging around him. To find out what problems lie in store for him, see the script in the box above."*

Cartoonman's first adventure
Rocketwoman is guiding her spaceship across the galaxy when the engine develops a fault. Forced to crash land on an unknown planet, she is besieged by alien lifeforms. Using his superhearing, Cartoonman learns of the danger. He speeds to the planet and soon has things sorted out. Returning Rocketwoman to her own planet, he receives a hero's send off and returns to base.

87

YOUR OWN CARTOON STRIP

When you've invented your superhero and developed a script, it's time to plan how to illustrate the action. In the best cartoon strips, the reader follows the plot, and also enjoys the strip as a visual adventure. Varying the size and shape of your pictures, or *frames*, changing the scale and perspective, all add to the impact of your tale.

A story in a single page
Sketch out some rough designs or *layouts* for your story. You only need to illustrate the main points, and leave the rest for the reader to imagine. Different frame sizes will be appropriate for showing key moments of action and for conveying necessary information.

Color is important. Different characters and locations should have different colors so that the reader can recognize them at a glance. Use strong colors for foregrounds, quieter colors for backgrounds.

When you're happy with your layout, fill in your frames, perhaps working in pencil at first and finishing off in ink and in color.

▷ **"Cartoonman's first adventure is illustrated on the opposite page. But you'll see I've used the speech bubbles to include some more tips on page layout. Can you imagine the actual words the characters would have used?"**

Laying out your page
Below are three sample page layouts. Try to see your page of cartoons as a single picture made up of different elements. Using only a small number of colors will help with this.

As these examples illustrate, cartoon frames don't have to be rectangular. Some images will fit better into a different shape. A diagonal line leads the eye on to the next frame; ovals and circles liven up the page. Experiment with your own alternatives, tracing round objects to get circles and curves.

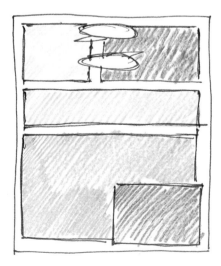

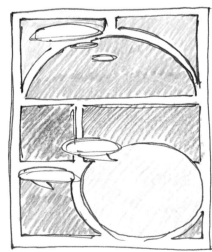

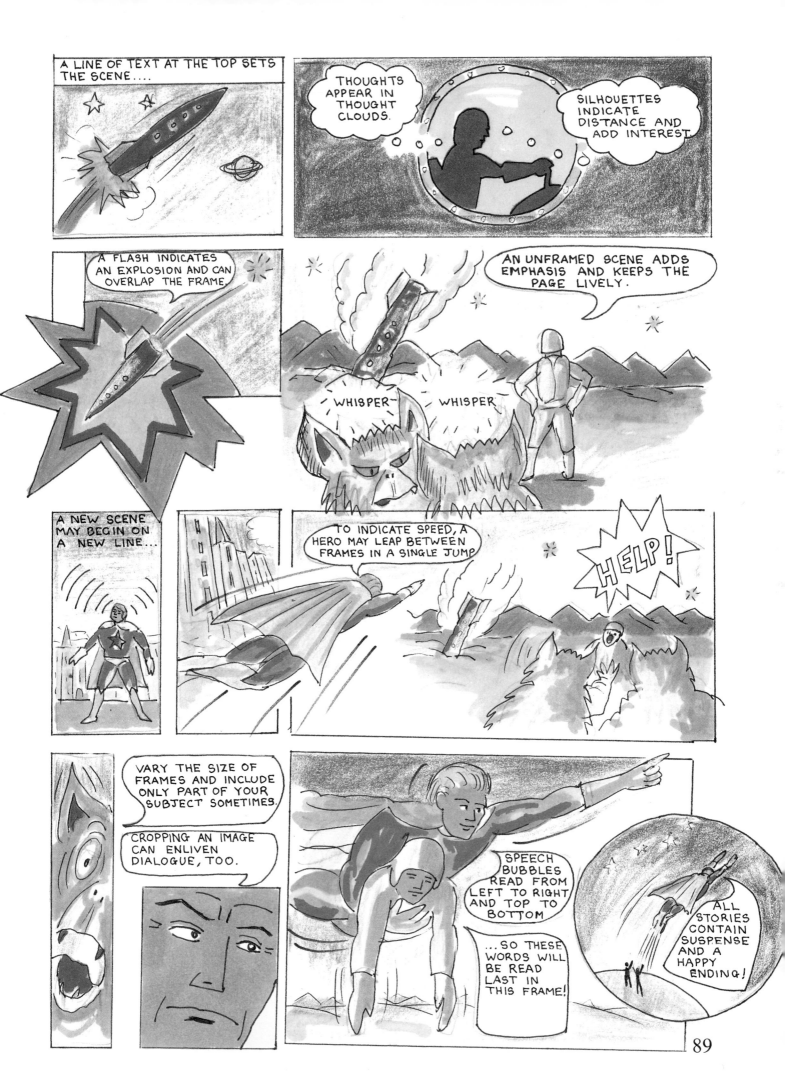

89

FLICK BOOK ANIMATION

The art of making pictures move is called animation. This need not be technical – it can be as easy and effective as the projects here.

Making a two-page flick book
The simplest form of animation is the flick book (below). All you need to make this is a pencil and a long strip of paper about three inches wide. The paper should be thin enough to see through, but should not be too fragile. Fold the strip in half, crease it and open it out again.

Before and after
Think of an action or event you want to illustrate, involving "before" and "after" positions. Draw the first stage of your idea on the second page of the two-page "book." In the example below, this is the man with smooth hair. Fold the first page of the book back over the image. You should be able to make out something of the picture underneath.

For your flick book to be effective, some parts of your image should remain the same. Trace these through the paper, then draw in the different parts that will appear to move.

Trial run
Once you've drawn your second picture, roll it up tightly around a pencil. Hold the paper down as shown at the bottom below. Then run your pencil left and right, to reveal your "before" and "after" pictures alternately.

Sample flick books
Below are two other "before" and "after" ideas. How about before and after going on vacation, using a hair restorer or taking a weight-loss pill?

Animated notebooks

Now try a further sequence of action. You'll need a notebook with blank pages of thin paper. Think of an action, and decide how many stages you need to illustrate it – the example shown uses nine.

Draw the key stages in your note book first, pages 1, 5, and 9 shown here, starting on page 9 with the last in the sequence. Trace the unmoving parts of the picture through the paper. Then fill in the pictures in between, again working from the back of the book.

▷ *"When all your stages are complete, flick the pages of your notebook and watch your picture come to life! The more accurate your tracing is, the more effective this will be."*

91

MOVING PICTURES

If you had the power to slow life down, you might see all movement as a series of tiny changes. The project here is about seeing complex action in this way. It will help to develop the skill of seeing as an animator does – in slow motion, one step at a time.

In your mind's eye

Think of a sequence of action like the one below, involving your superhero perhaps. As in the second flick book project, you will need to concentrate on the key moments of action first. These are your *key frames*, the beginning and end of the movement, and two or three other stages that sum up what is going on.

Once you're happy with your key frames, you'll need to sketch in the action in between (in pencil in the illustration below). These stages are known as "in-betweeners." You can choose to use tracing paper to reproduce the parts of your drawing that remain the same, and even the parts that look the same but have been moved to a different position.

Key frames and in-betweeners

In the cartoon industry, teams of illustrators are employed to produce action sequences. Artists working on full-length cartoon films use the system of key frames and in-betweeners. Only the key frames are drawn by an animator, leaving an artist, also called an "in-betweener," to fill in all the others.

▽ *"Not too easy for you and me, perhaps, but anything is possible in the world of animation. The four key frames are shown in color, and the in-betweeners are inserted to complete the sequence."*

Using a light box

Professional animators draw on sheets of transparent plastic called acetate. For tracing the parts of the image which remain the same in the next frame, animators use a light box (below). The completed sheet is pegged in position. A second sheet is laid on top. When the light box is switched on, the first image can be seen clearly, and parts of it traced.

Animation

Have you any idea how many separate pictures are needed for a full-length cartoon film? Hundreds? Thousands, perhaps? In fact, it's nearly a million. All this work used to be done by hand. Today, some of it can be done by computers.

Once a cartoon image is finished, it is photographed individually and becomes one frame of the film. There are 24 of these frames in one second of film time. When the film is shown in a theater, the frames change so fast that what we see is nonstop action.

▽ *"An animator uses a light box to see the outlines of a cartoon more clearly."*

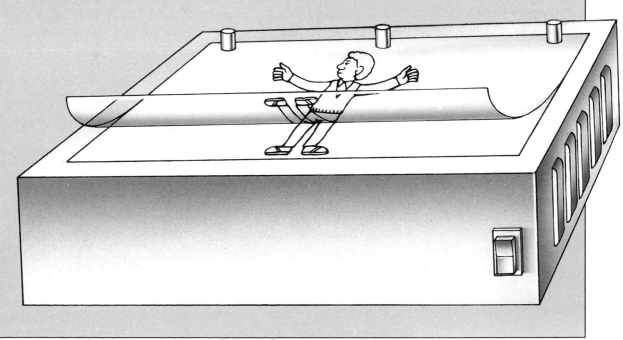

CARTOON PROJECTS

Some of the techniques explored in this book can be used to make presents for your family and friends.

Your own comic
Aim high by publishing your own comic book. Include all your best jokes, and the exploits of your cartoon strip heroes. Invent adventures with plots to be continued in the next issue; your friends will soon be clamoring for the next edition. Why not combine efforts with a friend or two? You could even try drawing a cartoon strip with a friend, doing alternate pictures and making it up as you go along.

Cartoon cards
Many of your drawings will make great cards. Your best two-frame joke, with the first picture on the front and the punch line inside, will work well.

Caricature cards are another possibility, but be careful who you send them to! On the left you can see someone receiving a caricature birthday card with mixed feelings.

Your favorite flick books can also make excellent cards. You could even include a pencil and instructions. The front page of your flick book must be on thin paper, or it won't roll around the pencil. For the other cards you could choose to work on thicker paper or cardboard, so that your finished product will stand up. Or you can cut out your cartoons and stick them onto cardboard with glue.

PRACTICAL TIPS ON CARTOONING

Protecting your equipment
Keeping your drawing equipment safe is important. Store your paper, pencils and drawing pads together in one place. This will help from a practical point of view, and give you a feeling of continuity in your work. Protect your paper by storing it away in a drawer where it can lie flat and will not get creased or soiled when it is not being used.

Getting rid of mistakes
Even professional cartoonists make mistakes. Erasers, of course, take care of errors in pencil. If your drawing is in a more permanent medium like felt-tip, tracing is a good way of saving the parts you're happy with. Thin paper like typing paper is easy to see through and trace with. Hold other kinds of paper against the window to see the drawing beneath.

Tracing is slow and careful work, and can inhibit you if your style is free and spontaneous. Your art store will stock small pots of opaque white watercolor which you can use to paint out any errors. New lines can be drawn in over the top.

Alternatively, you could cut a fresh piece of paper to cover your mistake and paste it over the top with glue. Mistakes on acetate can be sponged off with water.

Working with felt-tips
Felt-tips are excellent color tools. Use them to fill in areas of paper quickly and evenly. When you finish using a color, it's important to put the cap back on, or it will have dried out by the next time you need it! Remember that felt-tips soak through thin paper, so don't have anything precious underneath.

Stick mostly to light colors, and use strong ones mainly for detail. To some extent, felt-tips can be laid down over one another to create new colors. When not blending colors, allow time for one color to dry before applying another next to it, otherwise your work may smudge.

Fixative
If you're working with charcoal or conté, you will need to seal your work with fixative to prevent it from smudging. Cans are available from art stores. Place your finished drawing in a well-ventilated area and spray fixative back and forth over it. Be careful not to get any in your eyes.

The dictionary game
Coming up with ideas for cartoons, particularly for cartoon jokes, is easier for some of us than others. One exercise which can encourage the flow of ideas is the dictionary game. Get a dictionary and pick two words from it at random. Think up a way of linking them in a picture. If nothing springs to mind, try another word, but don't cheat too much!

CHAPTER FOUR: COLLAGE

Collage, a French word meaning pasting or gluing, is a very flexible art form. It can take you beyond the limitations of paints and brushes, and introduce you to a new world of creative picture making.

Everyone can do it

Collage can be quick and easy. It makes use of ready-made materials like photographs and colored paper, and is good for anyone who enjoys making images. You don't have to be a great artist to produce spectacular results. Collage can go hand in hand with drawing and painting, or can be a separate activity in its own right.

New from old

Collage is cheap. Rather than demanding expensive new equipment, it makes use of things people often think of as garbage. The materials you need are all around you and can cost next to nothing. Collage is about combining familiar things in new and original ways.

This chapter begins with a guide to tools, techniques, and materials. With the aid of projects, it guides you through simple image-making to a series of more advanced techniques.

▷ *"Scraps of styrofoam and candy box paper suggested this snow scene. I used corrugated cardboard for the house and string for the plants and broomstick. I laid bubble wrap packing material over blue paper to get the effect of falling snow."*

TEARING AND CUTTING

The next pages introduce some basic tools and techniques for paper collage. To get paper to the shape you require, you will need to tear or cut it. There are many different ways of accomplishing even this first step.

Tearing

It is very simple to pick up a piece of paper and tear a shape out of it. A torn edge can look very nice, both on its own or when placed next to a cut edge. Torn paper can often look surprisingly effective, once you've placed it in position. For more hints on tearing techniques, see the Practical Tips on page 125.

Cutting

The main tools for cutting are scissors and craft knives. Scissors are relatively safe and easy to control. Used skillfully, they can produce a variety of curved and straight lines.

A craft knife can be used to cut lines more freely. Used with care, a knife can cut shapes in paper as easily as a pencil can draw them. A craft knife is sharp. Cut away from your body, and be careful not to cut your other hand, which is holding the paper down. Always make sure the safety cover is replaced after use.

A cutting surface

If you're using a craft knife, you will need something to cut on. Cardboard will do, but it must be thick. Rubber cutting mats are quite expensive, but will never wear out.

Most paper is colored on both sides — the blue figure is from paper of this kind. When this paper is torn, some of the edges will be a lighter shade and have a different texture. Try this yourself with cheap colored paper.

Some paper is colored on one side only, and is white on the back. The figure in pink is torn from paper of this kind. Try tearing a piece in half yourself. One of your torn strips will have a colored edge, and one will be edged with a dramatic white line. This can look very effective against a background of a different color.

△ A hole puncher can be used to create interesting effects. Here, holes in blue paper create the effect of falling snow.

▽ Special scissors called pinking shears create a regular V-shaped edge, which can look like grass.

△ A craft knife makes clean lines. It is also good for cutting holes in the middle of paper, like the castle windows above. Remember to cover the blade after use.

▷ Folding or curling can make flat paper three-dimensional. The steps above were folded and the bird's plume was curled around a pencil. A torn straight edge can be created by tearing paper against a ruler. Scissors or a craft knife can be used to fringe paper or cardboard.

SPECIAL EFFECTS WITH PAPER

Paper is a very flexible material that can be used in all kinds of different ways. Some of the special effects you can achieve are described here; you may be able to think up some new ones of your own.

Changing texture

Paper usually has an even, uniform surface. But this **texture**, or feel, can be changed. Thin paper, such as tissue paper, can be crumpled and then flattened out again. Paper can also be pressed onto rough or textured surfaces to give it a different feel. This effect will be increased if you rub over the paper placed on a textured surface with a hard object like the back of a spoon.

With tin foil you can create the impression of an object by wrapping foil around it and then lifting it off. The spoon below is an example.

▽ *"The collage below uses a number of techniques to produce a picture of the objects found on a kitchen table. I crumpled purple tissue paper to imitate the wrinkled surface of prunes. To simulate the pitted surface of strawberries I pressed red paper over a sieve and rubbed it with a spoon. Sometimes the best way of capturing the look of an object is to include the object itself in your collage! The paper plate is an example."*

100

STICKING PAPER DOWN

Drawing and painting
Because it uses colored paper, one of the advantages of collage is instant access to large areas of color. You can also draw or paint parts of the paper to create a range of different effects. Colored pencils, crayons, chalks, felt-tip pens and paint can all be used for this.

Gluing paper down
Once your paper is torn or cut and painted, you will need to attach it to the background of your collage. Gluing is the basic method. Glue is available in liquid, paste and spray form, in pots, tubes or cans.

Different glues are right for different jobs. Most dry to a clear surface, and glue left showing can be rubbed away.

Tape, pins and staples
Tape can be used to stick paper down. Use double-sided tape on the back if you don't want it to show. Pins and staples can attach heavier papers to cardboard or styrofoam.

▽ *"Below is a fruit bowl collage made with a combination of cut and torn shapes, painted and stuck down in various ways. Thumbtacks and staples can become part of the picture – here I've positioned them to look like pips and stalks of fruit."*

101

THE WORLD OF PAPER

Paper is the single most important resource of the collage artist. From tissue paper to newsprint, from picture postcards to typing paper, it's important to get to know the range of papers that are available.

A library of paper

Start your own paper collection. You may be surprised by how much normally gets thrown away. Gather together a stock of paper that you can draw on for this project.

The aim is to find out what paper can do by putting together your own collage of flowers from different papers. Bring in as many textures as you can find. Sandpaper, envelopes and foil are used on the right.

Cut or tear yourself a series of petal shapes from your papers.

Practicing composition

If you pick or buy a bunch of flowers, you will probably want to arrange them in a vase at home. In the same way, your paper flowers need to be arranged in a pleasing way. This process is called composition. One of the great advantages of collage is the ability to practice composition, trying your materials in all kinds of positions before deciding on a final version. When you decide what looks best, stick them down.

▷ *"Don't forget you can overlap some of your flowers, as I have in the collage on the right. You'll find that using similar shapes will bring out the different qualities and textures of the paper."*

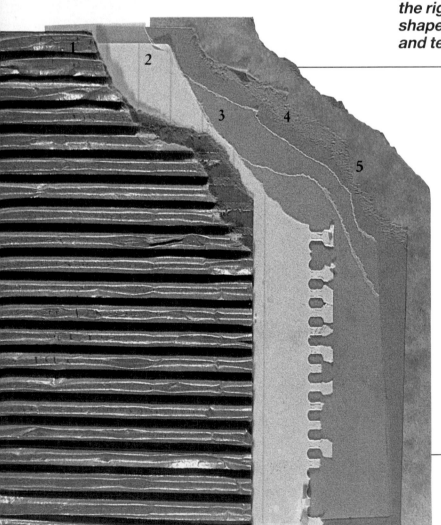

All about paper

Paper comes from trees. It's made from pulped wood mixed with water and pressed flat. Paper can have other substances, flax for example, mixed in with it to give it a different texture. Paper is available in many different weights and textures. Shown here are (1) corrugated paper (2) notepaper (3) tracing paper (4) construction paper and (5) wrapping paper. Construction paper is inexpensive and comes in many colors. Thick watercolor paper and cheap bond paper are also useful.

STEP BY STEP

Gathering your materials
The previous page explored the potential of paper in collage.
But collage can also involve a much wider range of materials. This project is about working with more varied materials, and building a picture with them step by step.

Begin by assembling your raw materials. You might collect ready-made images, like postcards and photographs from magazines. You could also include construction paper (shown behind the magazine photographs on the right).

1

△ *"A mixture of torn and cut edges will add interest to your picture. Your paper shapes can be overlapped. Keep an open mind about where and at what angle the pieces might go."*

2

△ *"Magazine images add color and texture to your work. Remember that being able to make alterations to your pictures before or even after sticking them down is an advantage of collage."*

◁ **"Here are some of the materials I used for the jungle collage. I added some interesting odds and ends – bits of packaging material, small toys and other scraps of junk that would otherwise have been thrown away."**

Finding a subject

If you are the sort of person who finds it easy to have ideas, a subject for your collage may come to you before you begin gathering your materials. Alternatively, as you make your collection, a theme that pulls them together may become clear. Sometimes it's easier to let your subject suggest itself to you, than to have a fixed idea before you start.

To begin your collage, cut and tear simple shapes for some of the key elements your theme suggests (1). Begin experimenting with these elements in different positions.

Size and scale

Postcards and photographs (2) provide ready-made images which allow you to experiment with size and scale. In real life, objects that are close to us look large, and those that are far away look tiny. You can recreate this effect in your collage with images of different sizes.

Look at the images of animals on the left. The largest, the lion, seems to belong in the front, or foreground, of the picture. The medium-sized gorilla looks right in the middle, and the tiny bird looks best at the top, where it appears to be in the distance.

Putting it all together

Now that your main materials are assembled, it's time to see how everything fits together (3). The elements of your collage are pieces of a puzzle that can be put together in different ways. There's no right or wrong way to assemble the pieces – it's about what looks best to you.

In the final stages, bring in the odds and ends of junk you collected earlier. These will add touches of interest, realism or even humor to your collage, and, most important of all, give it a three-dimensional look.

3

△ **"Above is the finished collage. A bottle top has become the sun, and a piece of string has turned into a snake sunning itself on a rock. A stronger glue was needed to fix these down securely."**

WORKING WITH COLOR

One of the joys of collage is being able to work with large areas of color, without first having to mix paint, or to crayon laboriously. There's no better way to find out how colors work together.

Colors have many jobs to do

Colors express feeling; they can create mood and atmosphere. Colors can blend together or stand out against each other. Colors influence one another; they can appear to change, depending on the other colors they are placed next to.

Colors can also suggest distance and space. Warm colors such as yellows and reds seem to jump out and grab your attention. Cool colors such as blues and purples are more relaxing. By positioning colors correctly, you can create a real sense of depth in your work.

Creating depth with color

This project will work best with transparent paper of different colors. Tissue paper is ideal; it allows colors to show through one another, so two different colors can be overlapped to make a third color.

Discover how to put colors in their place by building up a land- or seascape. Begin by laying down broad areas of color. Use warm colors in the foreground, and cooler colors in the background. Overlap your colors to create more subtle shades, like the turquoise at the water's edge in the collage shown.

▷ *"To get the tissue paper to lie flat, I put small spots of glue on either end of the torn strips and smoothed them down. When the background was finished, I added the details of the sun, boat and the bathers, to focus the eye on the different areas of the picture. "*

Warm colors advance toward you. They are right for the foreground of your picture. Cool colors recede; they fit best in the background.

The eye is drawn to contrasting colors such as yellow and purple, which demand attention. Other contrasting pairs are red and green, blue and orange.

A single layer of transparent yellow or red paper laid over a white background looks pale and muted; a double layer looks darker and brighter. Red and yellow are overlapped to make orange, as you can see in the middle below.

EXPLORING TONE

What is tone? Tone is about how light or dark something is. Take away color, and tone is what is left. Tone gives shape and solidity to objects, by showing where light falls on them. Reproducing this effect will make your work look convincing.

This project is about practicing seeing tone by making a collage in newspaper. Your subject could be a still life, like the one shown here.

Tone and lighting

Arrange some objects into a still life. Look closely at it. There are two factors that affect the tones there: the actual colors of your objects – how light or dark they are – and the effect of light falling on them. For example, a pale highlight on a black jug could actually look lighter than a shadow on a white plate.

Matching tone

Study the effect of light on your arrangement and identify areas of tone in it. Match what you see with the black, gray and white tones of your newspaper. Cut or tear shapes from paper of the right tone, and slowly build up your picture.

▷ *"From the large black letters of the headlines to widely spaced lettering and small print, a newspaper contains all the tones you need for your still life. To make the job simpler, I put the background in first, and the paler shapes over it."*

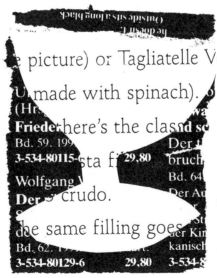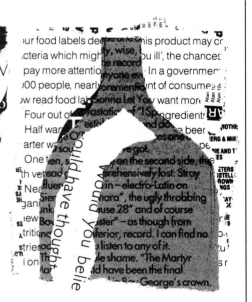

△ *"A light shining from the side creates areas of pale tone and shadow on an object. Sometimes these are very distinct."*

△ *"Placing light and dark tones next to one another produces a dramatic effect. The eye is drawn to these areas.*

△ *"Cut shapes convey abrupt changes in tone. A torn line can suggest one area of tone blurring into another."*

All colors have tones, too. If you look at the squares above, you may be able to identify particular colors, and the differences between their tones. Compare them to the tone of the page, and that of your hand holding this book.

MARBLING AND RUBBING

Marbling paper is fun, and can produce the most amazing results for you to use in collage. You will need oil paint, linseed oil, turpentine, a bowl and some jelly jars. Cover your working area with newspaper, and follow the instructions below.

Rubbings

Rubbings are impressions of textures in color. Look around you for objects with interesting textures. Place a sheet of thin paper over each, and rub the paper with colored crayon, pencil, or chalk.

▷ *"When you've produced a number of rubbings and marbled papers in different colors, study them and see what the different textures remind you of. Use them to make a collage, perhaps a landscape like the one on the right."*

△ *"In a jelly jar, mix up one teaspoonful of linseed oil with two of turpentine. Add six inches of paint squeezed from a tube, and stir the mixture with a stick."*

△ *"Make up several jelly jars with different colors. Fill a bowl with water. Pour in a jar of paint. The mixture will float on the surface of the water. Stir it again."*

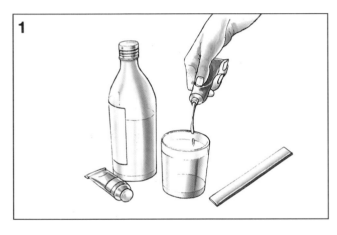

△ *"Take a piece of plain paper and gently lay it on the surface of the water. Lift it off again almost immediately, and let the excess water drain off. Lie it flat to dry."*

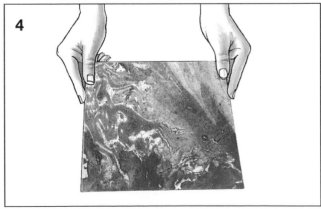

△ *"Your paper will now be marbled. You could immerse it again in a different color, or add a new color to the water and try again with a fresh sheet."*

Making a good impression
Below are some examples of different textures obtained by rubbing. Try rubbings of coins and the grain of wood.

Many kitchen utensils also have interesting textures – try a cheese grater, a sieve, and a straw place mat. You'll discover a new world at your fingertips!

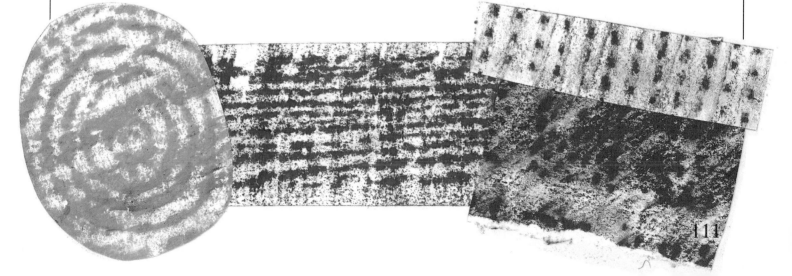

WORKING WITH PHOTOS

"From this day on, painting is dead." Many people believed this when photography was first invented. Artists today haven't actually given up painting, but a great many have used photographs in picture making.

Picture puzzles

Cutting up and reassembling a photograph is a little like making your own jigsaw puzzle. This process will produce a new image which can be intriguing, bizarre or funny.

You will need a collection of images from postcards or magazines. These pictures can be cut up, using scissors or a craft knife. Cutting paper with a craft knife held against a metal ruler will produce a clean edge. There are many ways in which the pieces that you cut can be reassembled. A few are shown here, and others are suggested for you to try.

Squares, strips and fans

Photographs can be cut into squares, as described below, or they can be cut into straight strips or curves. Curved strips can be spread out evenly, or shaped into a fan. Fanning will elongate your image. On the right, fanning has emphasized the curve of the goose's neck. This technique is very effective with photographs of figures in action.

Two into one *will* go

Another project with strips is shown at the bottom of the opposite page. This project works best with two images that complement each other, as the shape of the bird's head and the hill do there. Cut both pictures into strips, and intersperse the two images. When the pictures are combined, the shapes will interact with one another.

◁"The image on the left is composed of squares. To cut squares more accurately, mark out the lines on the back of your image first.
The illustration shows only one of the many ways in which the squares can be reassembled. Try rotating each square by 90°, and see what happens. Try again, rotating all the squares by 180° and sticking them upside down."

△ *"Here the photograph from the opposite page has been treated very differently. Try replacing strips like these in reverse order, or removing every other one and putting the rest together again."*

▽ *"The round hill echoes the shape of the bird's head below. Look for similar shapes for your own collage."*

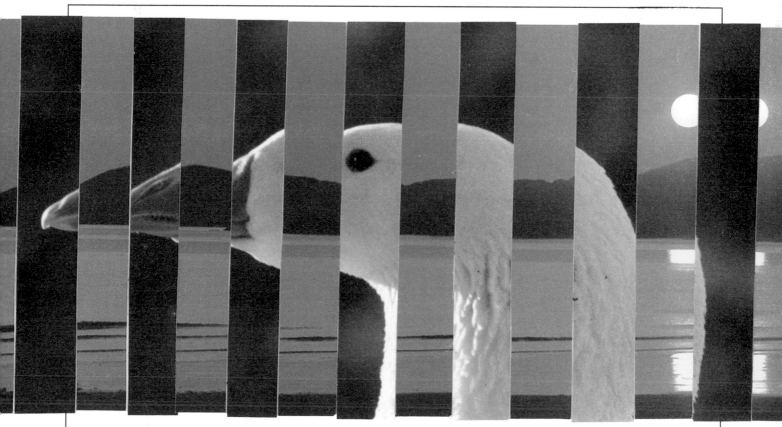

PHOTOMONTAGE

A collage made up of a number of photographs is called a photo-montage. Photomontages can often look more like pictures of dreams than of everyday life. In dreams, familiar objects or people are often transformed into the unfamiliar, and sometimes the same thing happens repeatedly. In photomontage, too, shapes can be repeated, and familiar images can be transformed into strange and bizarre ones.

This photomontage project is about exploring the patterns you can make with repeated shapes. You will need a craft knife and magazines.

Repeating shapes
Look through the magazines and find an image that appeals to you. Choose a figure or a simple form that is easy to recognize from its outline or silhouette alone. Cut around the outline, pressing down hard on the magazine and cutting through several other pages as you do so. When you've cut out your outline, you will be left with a series of identical shapes (see the illustration below).

Positive and negative
You will also have a number of holes in backgrounds – negative shapes –

Front and back
On the left below, the figure has been cut out and moved from its original setting, leaving the negative shape.

On the right, both figures and backgrounds have been turned over, to produce a series of shapes which mirror those on the left.

as well as the positive ones of the figure itself. The idea is to use these shapes as well in your collage.

Magazines are printed on both sides of the paper, so your positive and negative images will have parts of other pictures printed on the back of them. These, too, can become part of your picture.

Once you have a series of images and backgrounds, start to experiment with them. Turn some over and see how they mirror the others. Put them all together in your own collage. The montage below is based on this mirroring technique, and also on the dreamlike transformation of one thing into another.

▽ *"In my photomontage, single leaves have transformed themselves into whole trees. A cat's face has become a butterfly; its shape echoes the floating features of the face on the opposite side."*

DRAWING WITH COLLAGE

Your work so far may have involved a certain amount of drawing or painting on collage paper. This project is about quite the reverse – incorporating elements of collage into a drawing or painting of your own.

Using collage fragments

Choose a subject for a drawing or painting – it could be a street scene like the one shown here, or the view from your window, perhaps. Take a fresh look at the newspapers and magazines you gathered earlier. Get your imagination working on how these fragments fit in. Alternatively, let your fragments suggest a subject. Newspaper headlines, patches of newsprint and magazine advertisements can all find new homes – you can see these in the collage on the right. Don't take the words on your fragments too literally – they don't need to correspond exactly to your subject to fit in well.

Mixing materials

The picture opposite was drawn in pencil, charcoal, brown oil pastel, and pen and ink. You could use some of these in your own picture. Leave spaces in your drawing for your collage fragments. When you finish, glue them in place.

▷ *"If your subject is a street scene, printed words and pictures can add a touch of realism to storefronts, signs or billboards. Collage can also help you turn a drawing weak spot to your advantage. If you find drawing people difficult, why not collage them in instead?"*

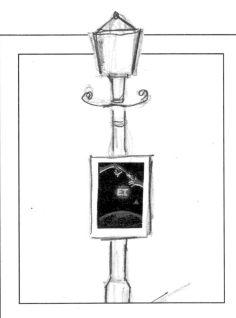

△ *"To avoid smudging, spray your drawing with fixative before you glue in your fragments."*

△ *"Alternatively, stick down your collage paper first, and draw an image around it."*

△ *"If you can't find a word, cut out separate letters and paste them down to spell it out."*

116

WORKING WITH FABRIC

You don't have to be able to sew or knit to enjoy the rich world of cloth. Fabrics open up an entirely new range of possibilities, enabling you to achieve effects you can't get any other way.

Many textures

Most households have a bag of cloth scraps tucked away. Collect as many different kinds of fabric as you can. Silk, corduroy, velvet, burlap, muslin – each material has its own unique character, a particular color, weave, texture and pattern.

Buttons, sequins, lace, yarn, and felt can all be brought in. You will also need a pair of sharp scissors, strong glue, pins or staples, and thick cardboard or cork to use as a base.

What do your scraps suggest?

Study your fragments and see what they remind you of. You could try a head like the one opposite, or an animal, landscape, or abstract pattern. Work as you have with paper, experimenting with your fragments in different positions before sticking or stapling them down.

▽ *"The odds and ends I collected suggested the crazy face and clothes of a clown. I chose pink nylon for the face and a background of cotton twill, and began by laying down these basic ingredients."*

▽ *"I chose shiny red cotton for the clown's nose, and small cotton patchwork squares for his jacket. I tried strands of yarn for the hair, but finally opted for a coarse tweed material."*

118

119

THREE-DIMENSIONAL COLLAGE

Throughout this book, in gluing one piece of paper over another, you have been creating an image which is actually three-dimensional. This project is about developing this quality fully, and creating an image that really stands out!

A load of old trash
You will need to make a new collection, this time of junk!

◁ **"Nails, pinecones, bark and the imprint of a car in foil have all been used on the left. The toys add interest and draw the eye to different parts of the collage."**

Old boxes, tubes, plastic bottles, toys, wood and leaves can all fit in. You will need a base of wood, cork or styrofoam. Nails, staples or glue can be used to fix objects to it.

Choose a subject or let your materials suggest one. You could try a science fiction city scene with stairways and towers, as shown here.

Using shadows
One of the advantages of 3-D collage is that the shadows cast by solid objects can become part of the design. When you're all finished, a coat of paint will unify your collage, and emphasize the play of light and shadow on it.

Adapting your materials
Some of your materials will need to be transformed before they can be used. Open out some boxes, cut into others; halve tubes and splay out plastic cups. Fold cardboard to make steps, cut doors and windows. Hide things inside others to be discovered at closer inspection.

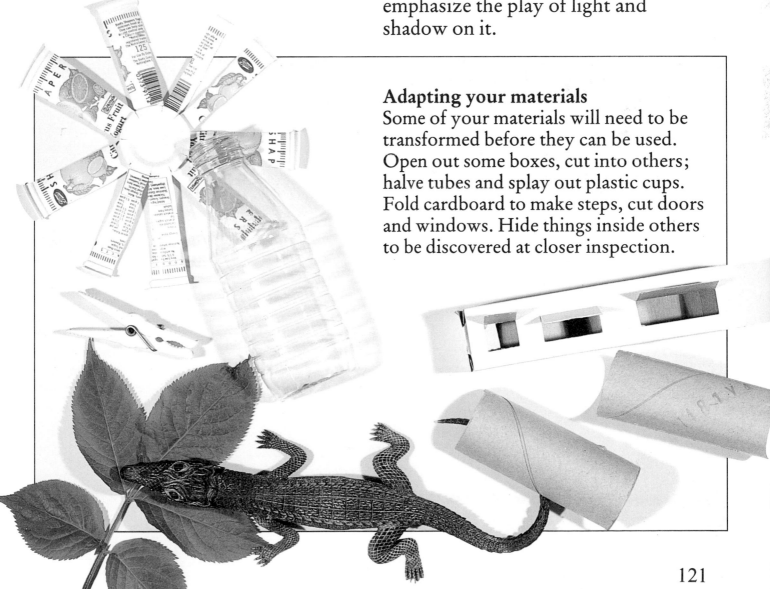

121

A DIARY IN COLLAGE

It's said that every picture tells a story. Have you ever kept a scrapbook of a vacation you went on, with all kinds of odds and ends that reminded you of the trip? This page is about using the bits and pieces connected with such a journey to make a collage. Again, the image you create will be three-dimensional.

Scrapbook journalism
In unknown territory, bus tickets and even candy wrappers can have a special magic. If you have an old scrapbook, this project provides you with an opportunity to recycle all your old vacation souvenirs. If not, you will need to go on a special expedition to gather your materials.

A trip to a gallery or museum, even a walk in the park can provide you with the inspiration you need.

On your expedition

Plan a journey in advance that is likely to yield the kind of materials you are looking for. On your trip, collect anything that might be effective in a collage, including tickets, maps, leaflets and postcards.

Take snapshots, or draw quick sketches. You could decide to stop regularly, every hundred paces for example, and note or pick up anything that looks interesting. The things you collect need not be just paper – balloons, coins, film and sand have all been used on the left.

Composing your materials

When you get home, arrange your materials on a large sheet of colored cardboard, or on a base of cork or styrofoam. Test out your objects in different positions. Try to plan another interesting journey, this time for the viewer's eyes as they wander over the surface of your collage. When you find the most pleasing composition, pin, stick or staple down your materials. Many modern artists have presented records of their journeys in this way.

◁ *"My collage records a trip to Disney World, but as you can see, the work is still in progress. Most of the materials have been positioned, but the objects bottom right have still to become part of the picture."*

Your own collage might include some of the materials below – brochures and postcards, maps, tickets and passes. You could also use "found objects" – twigs, leaves, flowers, earth, shells, and even packages of seasoning, as shown below.

GIFTS AND PRESENTATION

Collage offers a quick and easy way to produce all kinds of images in quantity. These images can make excellent cards and posters.

Repeating yourself
By pressing hard through several layers of paper with a craft knife, or by cutting several sheets at once with sharp scissors, you can create a series of identical shapes. These shapes can be used to mass-produce cards or posters. On the left are identical posters for a school play, which were made in this way.

Varying composition
Identical shapes don't have to be arranged in the same way every time. On the right are two party invitations made with identical materials. The pieces have been arranged in two very different compositions – shapes have been positioned at different angles, and even stuck in upside down. If you glue your paper shapes onto stiff cardboard, the final result will stand up and should last longer.

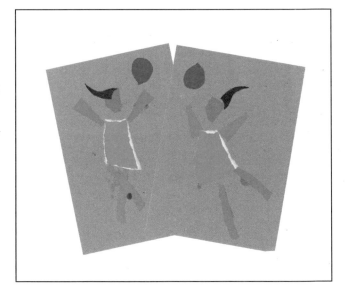

Presentation
Your collages will look even better when well presented. Some will look good with trimmed edges, mounted on cardboard or framed behind glass. If your collage is made of freely torn shapes, the rough edges may look best untrimmed, mounted with a border of cardboard on all sides.

PRACTICAL TIPS ON COLLAGE

Storing your materials

Many of the projects in this book have involved collecting materials. These need to be stored, if you wish to avoid the trouble of a time-consuming search every time you begin a new project. Organize some storage space for your materials. Sort different kinds of paper into separate piles, and file them away in a drawer if possible. If not, store them in boxes, trash can liners or plastic bags. If you can lie the bags flat, the paper will not get creased.

Preparation

You will also need to organize a work area. Whether you work on the floor or a table, you will need a lot of space. Collage is messy work, and in the heat of the moment, a certain amount of mess is inevitable. In fact, if you worry too much about making a mess, you probably won't be able to put so much enthusiasm into the project itself.

Before you begin, spread newspaper over the surface on which you intend to work. Wear old clothes. Keep tissues at hand to mop up spills or excess glue. Don't forget to replace the cap on your tube of glue, and to cover your craft knife when you have finished with it.

Gluing large areas

If you need to glue large areas of paper, wallpaper paste is ideal.

The paste should be mixed with water in an old bowl or jelly jar. You will need to apply it with a brush.

Warning

The fumes of some kinds of glue are harmful. Be very careful not to breathe them in.

More tearing techniques

Tearing is a direct and easy way of producing a shape in paper, but sometimes results may seem haphazard. You can achieve a more controlled tear by lightly scoring a line in your paper first with a craft knife or with the blade of your scissors. Tear along the scored line for a slightly ragged edge, or press out the shape instead.

Alternatively, draw the line you want with a paintbrush dipped in water, and then tear along it while the paper is still wet.

At a distance

Collages are pictures too, and they need the chance to be seen in their own right. Once your work has been framed or mounted, hang it on the wall where it can be seen from a distance. As you become familiar with your work over a period of time, you may notice things you want to change or reposition. One of the great advantages of collage is that additions and alterations are almost always possible.

GLOSSARY

Animation is the bringing to life of pictures; making them appear to move.

Caricature a drawing of an individual with exaggerated, or distorted features.

Complementary colors, in the art world are colors which are opposite eachother on the color wheel, and when next to eachother they are emphasized.

Depth gives a feeling of three-dimensionality. It shows distance and space within a design.

Foreshortening occurs when an object in a drawing, or painting is pointing directly at the viewer and the length of that object is hidden.

Gesso is a white primer used in preparing a canvas for painting. It can also be used to cover mistakes and unwanted blotches.

Hue is pure color without tone or brightness.

Layouts are simple and rough designs for a project, which illustrate only main points.

Linear perspective creates *depth* using two "parallel" lines which meet in the distance at the same

vanishing point.

Mounting is fixing a project to a setting, such as a stand or frame, to be ready for display.

Nibs, the attachments to the tips of ink pens. They vary in thickness and size for different types of lines.

Palettes are tools used in painting, for carrying paints and upon which to mix colors.

Pun, a play on words, that is often used in cartoons and comic strips.

Ready-made is a work of art created from found objects. For example, an old hat that has been decorated with plastic flowers.

Still life, a popular subject for many artist; they consist of a variety of inanimate objects, such as a bowl of fruit or vase of flowers.

Three-dimensional; something with *depth*, thickness and has a rounding out quality.

Vanishing point where two parallel lines, of the real world, meet on the horizon, in a diagram.

Viewpoint is the angle at which one is looking at an object or a scenery.

INDEX

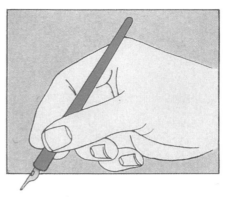